THE REMINISCENCES OF
Rear Admiral Oakley E. Osborn
U.S. Navy (Retired)

INTERVIEWED BY
Paul Stillwell

U.S. Naval Institute • Annapolis, Maryland

Copyright © 2002

Preface

This oral history came about fortuitously on the recommendation of Rear Admiral John Coughlin, who had served with Osborn in Patrol Squadron 17 in the late 1950s when both were junior officers. Since the Naval Institute's oral history collection had contained little up to now on the Navy's patrol plane community, the memoirs of both are valuable additions.

Oak Osborn grew up on a farm in the Midwest, but his destiny was changed in the mid-1950s when he and a friend spotted a recruiting billboard for naval aviation. Osborn went through the Aviation Officer Candidate School and subsequently became the first graduate of that program to become a Navy flag officer. Though he sought a billet in the TacAir side of naval aviation, the service's requirements sent him into patrol aviation instead. One of the points he emphasizes in this account is the parochialism that exists within naval aviation between TacAir and VP types.

In this oral history Admiral Osborn outlines the steps he took along the path to flag rank, moving from one patrol squadron to the next in assignments of increasing responsibility. He also served on two seagoing staffs that broadened his perspectives on antisubmarine warfare and ocean surveillance. Ashore he was in a variety of assignments, some within the framework of aviation ASW and others in more general areas, including joint-service billets. His final active duty was as deputy director of the Defense Mapping Agency.

A number of themes emerge as Oak Osborn recounts his life and service career. One is the idea of responsible service—that individuals should fulfill their assignments with integrity and be held accountable for their actions. Other themes are teamwork, learning, flexibility, aviation safety, the impact of weather on patrol plane operations, the importance of having a supportive family despite the difficulties of separation, and the satisfactions of the service life, particularly command. It is understandably a point of considerable pride with Admiral Osborn that two of his sons have become naval officers and thus carry the family tradition forward.

In what is a first for my experience in the oral history program, the interviewee, Admiral Osborn, did the initial transcription of his own interview tapes. Both he and I have done some editing in the interests of accuracy, smoothness, and clarity. In addition, I have inserted footnotes to provide further information for readers who use the volume. In going through the entire process of editing and footnoting, Admiral Osborn has been most cooperative.

Ms. Ann Hassinger of the Naval Institute's history division has made a significant contribution through her diligence in the overall process of printing, proofreading, and overseeing the binding of the completed volumes.

Paul Stillwell
Director, History Division
U.S. Naval Institute
November 2002

Biographical Summary of RADM Oakley E. Osborn USN (Ret.)

Born on a wheat farm near Dalton, Nebraska on October 25, 1933. Delivered by a midwife in the home farmhouse. Attended country school through eighth grade. Transport to school in all weather was by saddle horse. There were 8-15 total children in the eight grades. Attended high school in Sidney, Nebraska which was 20 miles away, graduating in 1951. My parents intended that I be educated in the finer points of agriculture and ultimately take over the family farm. Attained a bachelors degree in General Agriculture in 1955 after one year at the University of Nebraska and three years at Colorado State University. A draft deferment allowed completion of college.

Shortly after college graduation I volunteered for the U. S. Navy's new Aviation Officer Candidate program, which offered a commission after four months of pre-flight training - an attractive alternative to the draft and two years as a foot soldier. Commissioning was in February 1956, followed by completion of flight training and winging in March 1957. Pre-flight training was the most traumatic and uplifting experience I had known up to that time. Indoctrination under the heavy hand of two U. S. Marine drill instructors left impressions that stay with me to this day. The long, continuous road of military leadership development began with those dedicated Marines. Character building bestowed on me by my parents somehow carried me through the many unnerving experiences engineered by those DI's.

Flight training was an exciting and enjoyable experience as I adapted easily to the intricacies of flight. Two days after completing flight training, Catherine Heaton and I were married, a union that is 42 years and counting. Needless to say, Cathy was a Navy wife exceptional, guiding the early lives of four children as their father was deployed around the world.

First squadron, VP-17 at Whidbey Island, Washington, was a four year tour with deployments to Japan and Alaska. First Commanding Officer awarded me next-to-adverse marks for my professional efforts in a menial ground job. A later CO was mercurial in disposition, but fair and inspirational. I nearly left the Navy after this tour for airline flying. Assigned to a plumb position as instructor in the west coast replacement training squadron, VP-31, I was selected as one of four officers to commission the west coast training unit for the new P-3 Orion aircraft. During this tour I was co-pilot of the only Navy aircraft to fly non-stop from the U. S. to Japan without refueling, a feat that still stands.

Next assignment was as Aide and Flag Lieutenant for RADM Eli Reich, Commander Antisubmarine Warfare Group FIVE, aboard USS Bennington, CVS 20. He was relieved by RADM Turner F. Caldwell who was followed by RADM Robert MacPherson. Admiral Caldwell went on to be the first Director, ASW and Ocean Surveillance, OPNAV OP-095. This was a rewarding tour as I learned a great deal from three outstanding Naval leaders and their senior staff members.

Following tour was as Air Operations Officer on the staff of Commander Patrol Force, SEVENTH Fleet. The commander, RADM Roy Isaman, flew his flag from rotating seaplane tenders - USS Currituck, USS Salisbury Sound and USS Pine Island, and directed maritime patrol forces in the Seventh Fleet, which included P5M Marlin seaplanes, P3 Orions and P2 Neptunes. The tenders generally operated in the South China Sea or Camh Ranh Bay. Admiral Isaman was dual hatted as Commander Taiwan Defense Force with command of destroyers in the Taiwan Straits.

Next assigned to Navy Postgraduate School, With great difficulty and frustration I worked through a year in the Management curriculum and earned a Masters Degree in Personnel Management. This was followed by a tour as a department head and fleet pilot in VP-19 at Moffett Field, California. Attendance at the U. S. Army Command and General Staff College in Fort Leavenworth, Kansas in 1970-71 was a unique experience. The student body consisted of over 1100 officers including over 300 foreign officers. This was the height of the Vietnam war and the Calley trial was unfolding which lent an interesting air to the class discussions.

My first command tour followed in VP-40, first as Executive Officer and then Commanding Officer. I found this tour, and the command tours that followed, to be the easiest and most enjoyable experiences. Making command decisions was always a challenge but never a burden. Exposure to Washington, D. C. commenced with an assignment in OP-59 (CNO Aviation Directorate) under RADM Fred Koch. Early selection to Captain was followed by selection as Executive Assistant to VADM E. C. Waller, Director, ASW and Ocean Surveillance (OP-095). Duty in the heart of the E Ring opened a new world of exposure to Naval leadership and the challenges of the Pentagon bureaucracy.

Selection for major command and assignment as Commander Patrol Wing FIVE in Brunswick, Maine brought first time experience in the Atlantic Fleet. The major differences between the Atlantic and Pacific Fleets, both geographically and politically, became quickly apparent. This command entailed oversight of seven squadrons deployed at different times throughout the Atlantic and Mediterranean areas.

Return to Washington in 1980 brought new challenges and experience in personnel management. First assignment was as Director, Restricted Line and Staff Placement where all flavors of officer assignments were managed including doctors, dentists, lawyers, engineers, supply officers, chaplains, oceanographers and personal staff of all flag officers. This was followed by a period as Deputy to the Director of Personnel Distribution (NMPC-4). Selection to flag rank led to a short assignment as Director (NMPC-4). An interim assignment as Director of Total Force Training (OP-11) was followed by a tour as watch team commander in the National Military Command Center (NMCC). Leading a watch team in the NMCC was unique, exciting and broadening. Calling Casper Weinberger at 3 AM with bad news was a mixed experience.

The dream of an naval officer schooled in Maritime Aviation is to command the Atlantic or Pacific Patrol Aviation forces. I had the pleasure of serving as Commander Patrol Wings Pacific Fleet 1984-1986, a period of intense Cold War activity. The force consisted of fourteen squadrons, five air stations, eight Tactical Support Centers and approximately 5000 men and women. My reporting seniors during the period were Pete Easterling (COMNAVAIRPAC), Ken Moranville and Duke Hernandez (COMTHIRDFLT), and Ace Lyons (CINCPACFLT). Soviet submarine activity in the EastPac was intense, heightening in one period to the point that P3 aircraft were prosecuting six different Soviet submarines at the same time. Many leadership challenges arose during the tour including my convening a general court martial on a Commanding Officer for fraternization with a junior officer and prosecuting my staff Flag Secretary for sexual abuse with an adolescent. I saw aviation safety as a major issue in the fleet and placed significant emphasis on the issue.

Final tour was in the Defense Mapping Agency as Deputy Director. The Director was Major General Robert Rosenberg, USAF. He inherited a bureaucracy with 33 Senior Executive Service managers and 9000 men and women. The agency was transitioning from manual technique paper map making to a totally new digital process supported by satellite imagery. This transition was not unlike moving from a manual typewriter to a current technology computer. Bob Rosenberg is an aggressive, impatient manager who gives no quarter. His style was a shock to old timers of the agency. It happened that he was just what the agency needed, but the atmosphere was full of electricity. I played the role of mediator with mixed success. Here was a classic mix of military and government civilian management backgrounds and styles.

Retired in 1988 after over 32 years of commissioned service.

Biography - Chronological - Oakley E. Osborn (birth to completion of Naval Service)

1988	Retired from U. S. Navy
1986-1988	Deputy Director, Defense Mapping Agency
1984-1986	Commander Patrol Wings U. S. Pacific Fleet
1982-1984	Deputy Director Operations, National Military Command Center J-3, JCS
1982	Director of Training, Office of the Chief of Naval Personnel, OPNAV OP-01
1981-1982	Director Navy Personnel Distribution, Navy Military Personnel Command (NMPC)
1981-1982	Deputy Director, Navy Personnel Distribution, NMPC (selected to flag rank)
1980-1981	Director Restricted Line and Staff Placement, NMPC
1978-1980	Commander Patrol Wing FIVE
1976-1978	Executive Assistant to Director ASW & Ocean Surveillance, OPNAV OP-095
1974-1976	ASW Readiness and Training Officer, OPNAV OP-594
1972-1973	Commanding Officer, Patrol Squadron 40
1970-1971	Student, Army Command & General Staff College
1968-1970	Fleet Pilot, Patrol Squadron 19
1966-1967	Student, Personnel Management Curriculum, Navy Postgraduate School
1965-1966	Staff, Commander Patrol Force Seventh Fleet
1964-1965	Aide & Flag Lieutenant, Commander ASW Group FIVE
1963-1964	Flight Instructor, Patrol Squadron 31 Detachment Alpha
1961-1963	Flight Instructor, Patrol Squadron 31
1957-1961	Fleet Pilot, Patrol Squadron 17
1955-1957	Student Naval Aviator, Naval Aviation Training Command
1952-1955	Student, Colorado State University majoring in General Agriculture
1951-1952	Student, University of Nebraska
1947-1951	High School, Sidney, Nebraska
1939-1947	Grade School, Country school, Dalton, Nebraska

Born October 25, 1933 Dalton, Nebraska

Deed of Gift

The U.S. Naval Institute is hereby authorized to make available to individuals, libraries, and other repositories of its choosing the tapes and/or transcripts of two oral history interviews concerning the life and naval career of the undersigned. The Naval Institute may also, at its discretion, use the material in electronic/digital format, including posting on the Internet. The interviews were recorded on 31 March 2000 and 6 October 2000, in collaboration with Paul Stillwell for the U.S. Naval Institute.

The undersigned does hereby release and assign to the U.S. Naval Institute the rights and title to these interviews, with the exception that the undersigned retains the right to use the material for his own purposes, as he sees fit. The copyright in both the oral and transcribed versions shall be the sole property of the U.S. Naval Institute. The tape recordings of the interviews are and will remain the property of the U.S. Naval Institute.

Signed and sealed this __17__ day of __April__ 2002.

Oakley E. Osborn
Rear Admiral, U.S. Navy (Retired)

Interview Number 1 with Rear Admiral Oakley E. Osborn, U.S Navy (Retired)

Date: Friday, 31 March 2000

Place: United States Naval Institute

Interviewer: Paul Stillwell

Paul Stillwell: Admiral, it was a pleasure to meet you yesterday and get acquainted. Today we have embarked on an oral history of your naval service. If you could begin at the beginning please—something about your parents' background and where you were born.

Admiral Osborn: I was born on a farm near Dalton, Nebraska, October 25, 1933. The farm was about 10 miles from town and the nearest doctor. As was the practice in those days, most babies were born without the assistance of a doctor in farming communities. I think one of the neighbor ladies helped out. This was a bit of a problem, because I weighed over 12 pounds. My mother was 44 years old, so the birth was nearly the undoing of her. My father was born in eastern Iowa on a hog farm, and my mother was born in Council Bluffs, Iowa. She was mostly Danish background and my father mostly English.

My father moved to western Nebraska about 1911 and homesteaded. He lived in a tent and "broke" sod with a moldboard plow, living some very tough times. After a couple of years, he went back to Council Bluffs, married my mother, and brought her out to the new farm. They lived in very austere circumstances for several years while they were getting going. Eventually they built a new home, which stands today, and is the residence of my nephew, son of my sister, Ruth. He farms most of the land that my father had at that time.

Paul Stillwell: What were the principal products of the farm?

Admiral Osborn: The farm was what is known as a "dry land" farm, meaning total dependence on rainfall which averages about 20 inches a year. The grain, mostly wheat, was planted in the fall, came up the next spring, and was harvested in the summer. That ground was allowed to lie idle for a year to replenish nutrients, so only half the acreage produced each year. We also raised barley, oats, and corn—mostly as feed for the farm animals, rather than as a cash crop.

Paul Stillwell: What are some of your memories of growing up on the farm in Nebraska?

Admiral Osborn: Our farm was about 10 miles from town, and the closest neighbor was about a mile away. My pre-school and elementary school years were a bit lonesome, because there was no one nearby to play with. Also, the farm required a lot of work, and my father expected me to contribute. I didn't enjoy that aspect very much, but in retrospect it was probably the best thing that ever happened to me, because I learned how to do a hard day's work and stick to the job. Being born in 1933, I experienced the dust bowl years of the '30s. One particular dust storm stands out in my memory. We got up in the morning on a very quiet day. Looking to the west, we could see this giant brown dust cloud reaching into the sky as high as you could see and coming our way. When the storm hit, we were in total dust for several days. During the storm we tried to keep a damp rag over our faces to keep from breathing too much dust. When the wind finally abated there was ½ to ¾ inch of dust on the floor of the house. Fences 4 feet high were completely covered, just like a snow fence. It was a terrible experience and one I will never forget. This was also the time of the Depression.*

Paul Stillwell: How was the market for farm products during that Depression era?

Admiral Osborn: There was a time when my father had a good crop of wheat that he did not even carry to market, because it would cost him more to transport it than he would get

---

* Following the crash of the New York Stock Exchange in late October 1929, the United States was plunged into the Great Depression, from which it did not recover until the nation geared up for World War II at the beginning of the 1940s. The Depression was marked by high unemployment and many business failures.

paid for the grain. Those were very lean times, and at that time he had a very extensive acreage. I think he had about 4,000 acres. This is the equivalent of over 10 square miles of land. In order to save the farm, my father had to let part of his land go to the mortgage bank. He let the least productive land go—at least he thought it was the least productive. Several years later oil was discovered on the land that he had released.

Paul Stillwell: You mentioned your sister. Did you have other siblings?

Admiral Osborn: Yes, I had three sisters and one brother. One sister, who is 87, survives. My other sister was killed in a car accident this year. My brother, Clif, graduated from high school in 1943 and immediately joined the U.S. Marines. He went to battle at Iwo Jima in February 1945.* He went ashore in the ninth wave as a light artilleryman but quickly became a rifleman and was fortunate to survive the 33-day battle with light wounds. After the war Clif came home to the farm and ran a farm machinery business with my brother-in-law. Eventually he decided he wanted to be a Lutheran minister. With responsibilities of a wife and two children, he got his college degree and completed seminary requirements. Unfortunately, at one of his churches he got to be quite friendly with the church secretary. The two of them split with their mates and got married. He was asked to leave the church.

One event was quite significant to me, and I am sure it was to him. During the Vietnam War, Clif decided to harbor draft dodgers in his church in western Kansas. He became quite vocal and quite visible on the issue. This so infuriated me that we did not speak for five or six years. We eventually did get back together before he died of a heart attack several years later. My sisters were all gone from home in my days of youth, so I didn't spend a great deal of time with them or know them well at that time. They all married and had children and very productive lives.

---

* On 19 February 1945, U.S. Marines invaded the island of Iwo Jima, approximately 660 miles south of Tokyo, and captured it in a fierce campaign. The objective was to provide a forward airfield—an emergency landing site—to support the U.S. bomber offensive against Japan.

Paul Stillwell: Did your brother's example in the Marine Corps provide a source of inspiration for you?

Admiral Osborn: I don't know if it did at the time. I suppose it did to a degree. After I got into the Navy, I had a lot of feelings about that and had a really strong desire to go to Iwo Jima, but was never able to get there for one reason or another. In 1994 I had the privilege of traveling to Iwo Jima. We had gone to Yokosuka to visit our son who was stationed there, and I was able to arrange a flight to the island. The beach is just like it was the day they invaded. There is a wall about 10 or 12 feet high of volcanic sand, which is nearly impossible to climb. You can easily visualize the crossfire onto the beach from Suribachi and the northern part of the island. They had carefully placed their guns so that they could have a perfect crossfire on the beach. They knew exactly where the Marines were going to have to come in. To stand on that beach and visualize the landing and slaughter of U.S. Marines was one of the strangest feelings you can imagine.

Paul Stillwell: Was it an emotional experience?

Admiral Osborn: Very emotional. I stood there on the beach for nearly a half hour transfixed. I had, not too long before that, read the book Iwo Jima, by Bill D. Ross, an excellent work written by a correspondent who was in the thick of the battle the entire time.[*] After the time on the beach we went to the top of Mount Suribachi. Standing where the famous flag raising took place, followed by a tour of the island, was an experience very difficult to describe. I only hope that my children and grandchildren will take the time to read Iwo Jima and Flags of our Fathers by James Bradley in order to get a sense of what my brother and all World War II military went through to save our country from foreign domination.[†]

Paul Stillwell: You described it as lonely growing up. What sorts of things did you do for amusement during those years?

---

[*] Bill D. Ross, Iwo Jima: Legacy of Valor (New York: Vanguard Press, 1985).
[†] James Bradley with Ron Powers, Flags of our Fathers (New York: Bantam Books, 2000).

Admiral Osborn: I liked to hunt, did a lot of hunting. During my elementary school years I rode a horse to school, which was about four miles from home. I ran a trap line and would check my traps on the way to and from school. Trapping was mostly skunks and badgers. This sounds like strange amusement, but it was my amusement and my enjoyment. One day on the way to school I was sprayed by a skunk that was in a trap. When I arrived at school the teacher immediately sent me home to get socially acceptable.

I had one friend who lived about a mile away and we played together, although his father kept him pretty busy also. When I became old enough to drive, my father often sent me to town for parts and supplies. I had friends and acquaintances there from church and always enjoyed going to town. I loved baseball and listened to major league games on the radio nearly every day. The announcer was Gordon McLendon. I learned years later that he was not at the games but announced and provided sound effects while reading the ticker tape sent from the stadium. I loved sports but was not a very good athlete. Baseball was the favorite, and I played with several area teams. I never played football. Our high school had football and track and basketball.

Part of the reason I didn't get involved in high school sports was because I drove 20 miles to school from the farm and had to get home each afternoon to help with farm work and chores. Chores consisted of milking cows, feeding the cows, pigs, sheep, and chickens and mucking out the pens in the barns. Often I would relieve my father on the tractor in late afternoon and go until dark.

Paul Stillwell: I remember hearing of rural electrification. When did that come?

Admiral Osborn: That came around 1950 through the Rural Electrification Administration. It was a very significant event in our lives, believe me. It was like a miracle to have electrical power and indoor plumbing. It seemed like a miracle because during the years prior to REA we had no water or electricity in the house. It was my job to carry water from the well outside to supply our needs. We had an outhouse which was located about 50 yards from the house. Western Nebraska can be pretty harsh in the wintertime. Many days the seat of the outhouse was covered with snow. We used Sears & Roebuck catalog paper for toilet paper; they used pretty good paper in those days. The combination was memorable. About 1945 my father had a 32-volt Wincharger installed on the farm. It was a wind-driven generator on a high tower which supplied a series of very large batteries in the basement. This arrangement was strictly for light with no appliances. We used an icebox with blocks of ice up until we got REA. We eventually got TV with one channel—sometime in the '50s. The picture was very snowy due to our distance from the TV station.

Paul Stillwell: How good a student were you?

Admiral Osborn: Well, I was a pretty good student, at least according to my grade-school teacher. I did fairly well in high school. I didn't study very much. The grade school was a one-room schoolhouse four miles from the farm. There were somewhere between 10 and 13 total students among the eight grades. My teacher was outstanding. She entered me in the countywide spelling contest, which I won for my grade. I was very good in English. My high school teachers were also excellent, particularly my English teacher. She was an old shrew disciplinarian and never cracked a smile, but she drew my attention for some reason and gave me a good English language base. The other students hated her because she was extremely strict. A group of five of us became close in high school and keep in touch to a degree today.

The plan was for me to take over the family farm, so my father sent me to agricultural college after high school. First year was at the University of Nebraska, the last three at Colorado A&M (now Colorado State University).[*] I spent a good share of my time in college doing other things besides studying.

Paul Stillwell: Why was that?

Admiral Osborn: I don't know. I suspect that I really wasn't all that interested in the subject matter for one thing. I did what I had to and got a few A's, mostly B's, and

---

[*] The school is in Fort Collins, Colorado.

occasionally a C. But, I never applied myself. I had too many friends who liked to fool around and do other things.

Paul Stillwell: You must have felt like you were liberated when you got to go away to college.

Admiral Osborn: It was a totally different world.

Paul Stillwell: Wouldn't a college-educated farmer be an exception in western Nebraska in that era?

Admiral Osborn: I don't know about exception, but certainly minority. My father was a very forward-looking professional. He pioneered a number of farming techniques that the neighbors laughed at. Those were the kind of techniques that became the new agriculture and the new way to treat the soil. His farming methods were revolutionary for the time and later became the standard in soil conservation. He was an inventor of sorts. He was constantly modifying his machinery to work better. Of course, I was involved in that, and I think a little rubbed off on me.

Living on the farm was not much fun at the time, but as an adult it became clear to me what a wonderful way it was to grow up. Probably the most important thing was that I learned how to do a day's work and the feelings you get from doing a hard day's work. Working 15 or 16 hours physically and being so tired that you just wanted to lie down and not eat supper. There is something about that feeling that is unique, and I suppose there was a feeling of accomplishment, because the times we did that were usually during harvest time. The whole year on the farm is geared to harvest. Harvest is the climax. When you get to that point and the harvest is successful, it is the whole story. The feeling of accomplishment of being involved in that and being a part of it was very exhilarating.

When I was old enough to drive, my father had me driving a truck hauling the wheat from the combines in the field to the granary. I loved to drive. He started me driving a truck when I was about nine or ten years old. I was given responsibility beyond my years. At age 12 I was driving a truck on highways, which produced several citations from the state patrol for driving under age. My father would pay them and put me back on the road, because he didn't have a lot of options for farm labor.

Paul Stillwell: Farm life certainly inculcates a sense of discipline.

Admiral Osborn: Absolutely. I look at our children, and now our grandchildren and the young people of the nation today. Very, very few of them have had the opportunity or been forced to do a full day's manual labor. They don't have any concept of what that means. I think that is unfortunate.

Paul Stillwell: Did romance or dating start somewhere in all this process?

Admiral Osborn: Not until I got to college—well, a little bit in high school. I was a farm kid in a town. There were 71 in my high school graduating class, so our high school was like 400 total, and I was a real farm hick. The good-looking girls were taken up by the town boys. I did a little dating in high school, but I really didn't start dating much until college. I had one serious girlfriend in college. My wife Cathy and I met after I joined the Navy. She was actually from the town where I went to high school. I was in advanced flight training in Hutchison, Kansas, and drove home to Nebraska for the weekend and met her. I had known who she was, but she didn't know me. We met in December of 1956 and were married on St. Patrick's Day 1957, a few days after I became a naval aviator. Obviously, we were in love!

Paul Stillwell: Please tell me how you migrated from this agricultural course into the Navy.

Admiral Osborn: Migration from agriculture to the Navy was by happenstance. I held a college deferment from the draft but was due to be drafted into the Army upon graduation. A few days before graduation a friend and I were driving to Denver from Fort Collins, Colorado, for the weekend and saw a billboard by the highway announcing a new Navy flight program for college graduates called the Aviation Officer Candidate Program. We went to the recruiting station in Denver, where the officer in charge immediately identified a couple of "fish." Neither of us had the least idea of what we were getting into. I had never been in an airplane. The program offered a commission at the end of four months of pre-flight, followed by flight training.

We took a written exam, and then the recruiter said we needed to go flying to see if we were aeronautically adapted: "I'll take you up in a plane and we'll fly around and see how that works." The day of the flight we went to NAS Buckley east of Denver.* The recruiting officer took us up in an SNB, twin-engine Beechcraft. The day was typical for the Denver area in the summertime. The airflow over the mountains creates significant turbulence. This caused me to get airsick immediately after takeoff, and I never get an opportunity to take the controls. On landing he announced that we were both aeronautically adapted, and from there we completed the entrance requirements.

Paul Stillwell: That billboard changed your life.

Admiral Osborn: That billboard changed my life, definitely. I don't know if I would have thought about anything but the Army if I hadn't seen that billboard. It was just a happenstance. I certainly have never regretted that it happened. My father did. He had always expected me to take over the farm after college graduation. The Navy commitment was for four years, while the Army hitch would have been two years.

Paul Stillwell: What happened after you were determined to be "aeronautically suited?"

Admiral Osborn: We signed up in May of 1955 and went to Pensacola to report to preflight training in September 1955. That was an experience, to say the least. There were 77 of us in the class. Our class was the first full class of the new Aviation Officer Candidate (AOC) program. There had been one class previous that had half cadets and half AOCs. Preflight was a shocking and upside-down experience for a Nebraska farm boy. The two Marine drill instructors (DIs) set about tearing us apart and rebuilding us to

---

* NAS—naval air station.

their specifications. As years go by, I will forget many names of people I have known well, but never, never will I forget the names of those two DIs, Sergeants Reefle and Jones. We hated them, but at the end of the four months I respected them. They were both sharp guys. Reefle was very intelligent. Jones was not quite as smart, but he was just as good.

At any rate, I remember the first night in indoctrination battalion just like it was yesterday. They turned our world upside down, stripped everything away from us and started to rebuild us, and they didn't have much time to do it—four months. It's not like if they have a new Marine at Parris Island, where they can just have you.* They are dealing with college graduates who have to do a lot of other things during the day, so they have a tough time. They don't waste any time. I have often thought that both of these guys had families, and it seemed like they were there in the battalion with us every minute. They weren't, but it seemed like it. I don't know how they had any family life at all. Those guys were totally dedicated to what they were doing. I have never seen more dedication. They were pros in the truest sense of the word. We cadets got to know each other very well. Some of us are still good friends today. On the other hand, some of our classmates were a big disappointment. There were the odd one or two that were there strictly for themselves and didn't understand the team game.

Paul Stillwell: Was it a competitive environment?

Admiral Osborn: Yes, it was. Very competitive. On the other hand, the guys it was the easiest for, for one reason or another, tended to help guys it was hardest for. But it was still very competitive. I had learned to swim in college, but barely. Fortunately I had done that—one of the best things I ever did. The athletes in the class breezed through the obstacle course, but it was tough for me and many others. Everybody was encouraging everybody else. We had one gent who was absolutely petrified at jumping off a tower. You had to do that in the swimming pool and the obstacle course. His name was John Ennis. The day of the jump in the pool, he started off and changed his mind, caught hold

---

* Marine Corps Recruit Depot, Parris Island, South Carolina.

of a pole and hurt himself. This made matters worse, so when he got to the obstacle course we had to practically push him off the tower. The funny thing about that was, on his solo flight at Whiting Field, the engine quit, and he had to make a dead-stick landing.[*]

Paul Stillwell: You said this was a transition period from the old aviation cadet program to the AOC program. How did those two programs differ?

Admiral Osborn: The Naval Aviation Cadet (NavCad) program required two years of college. You went through the entire nominal 18-month flight training program as a cadet and were commissioned concurrent with receiving your Navy wings of gold. In our program you went through the four months of pre-flight training as a cadet, were then commissioned, and went through flight training as an officer. The AOC program was a much easier way of living, plus you received officer's pay, which was probably more important than the easier living.

Paul Stillwell: When the cadet program commenced in the '30s, the men would go to the fleet still ranked as cadets for a while before they got commissioned.

Admiral Osborn: Yes, and the cadet program continued on for quite a number of years after the AOC program came in. They still took in a lot of cadets for several years.

Paul Stillwell: You have undoubtedly seen the movie An Officer and a Gentleman, in which Lou Gossett plays the Marine drill instructor.[†] How true to life was that movie?

Admiral Osborn: It wasn't bad. I thought it was fairly accurate. They took license, but he did a good job as a drill instructor. Actually he won an Oscar for that. I was only reminded of that last night because our ten-year-old granddaughter is involved in a Black History program at the University of Maryland, and she had to memorize something like

---

[*] Naval Air Station Whiting Field, Milton, Florida.
[†] An Officer and a Gentleman was a 1982 movie that starred Richard Gere and David Keith as aviation officer candidates. The hard-bitten Marine Corps drill instructor in the film was Gunnery Sergeant Emil Foley, a character portrayed by actor Louis Gossett, Jr.

250 questions and answers. One of the questions was, "Who are the six black actors who have won Oscars, and what were the names of the movies?" One of those was Gossett for this movie.

Paul Stillwell: What was a typical day like in that program?

Admiral Osborn: We were up early, 5:00 or 5:30. The first thing was to ensure that your uniform was absolutely perfect, that your room and your belongings were in perfect order. We marched to the chow hall, where you only had about five minutes to eat. You picked up a tray, they threw the food on, and you sat down, but you never had time to eat it. We would then march for about an hour; then we went to class. We had four or five aviation-oriented courses. When classes were over we marched some more and did the obstacle course quite often. We swam daily and did an indoor obstacle course in an old hangar, as well as a lot of physical stuff. There was study period until about 9:00 o'clock; then lights out and back to it again.

Paul Stillwell: Any more on Officer Candidate School to relate?

Admiral Osborn: Yes, there is one thing. It kind of goes back to your article about Admiral Zumwalt in Naval History.* About a week after I was in pre-flight, I really wanted to get out of there; it just didn't seem like it was for me. I just wanted to get out.

Paul Stillwell: Was it homesickness?

Admiral Osborn: That probably had something to do with it. The regimentation. Did I want to live in this kind of environment? It was just so foreign to a Nebraska farm boy. You can't imagine anyone going in there that was less prepared. There were a lot of worldly guys in our class. We had guys like President Nixon's brother, who was in the

---

* Admiral Elmo R. Zumwalt, Jr., USN, served as Chief of Naval Operations from 1 July 1970 to 29 June 1974. The article that mentions his unhappiness as a plebe at the Naval Academy in 1939 is "Death of a Family Man," Naval History, April 2000, page 4.

next class.* We had a couple of guys who were wheeler-dealers and could manipulate the system, plus a host of others who had "been around." Here I am, a hayseed. At any rate, one night I went down to the office and requested permission to see the DI, which in itself was a pretty unnerving step. I can't remember exactly what he said, but he didn't take the fatherly approach. He berated me, embarrassed me, told me what a chicken I was: "Nobody is going to quit my program. I don't know what you are doing down here, but you are wasting your time. Now, get the hell out of here, go back up there, and do what you are supposed to be doing." So that was the end of that idea.

Paul Stillwell: Of course, he had been through this situation with many others and knew how to deal with it.

Admiral Osborn: He knew exactly how to deal with it. I was probably easy. Another observation. The day we got our commission and started flight training, over 30 of these 70 guys went to administration and "DORed"—dropped on request. They had this all figured out beforehand. These were guys who had been about to be drafted like I was. They knew from the start that if they went through pre-flight and got a commission, then DORed, their obligation was only two years. They spent two years avoiding the draft as public affairs officers, recreation officers, etc., in a nice environment in officer quarters on officer pay. Not long after, the Navy raised the bar to four years of service after commissioning and eventually raised it even higher. So there were a lot of "worldly" guys in the class. It was really quite a shock and disappointment, because among these 30 were some who seemed like pretty good souls. In my view they cheated the Navy, the government, and their country.

Thirty years later I was the guest speaker at our son Brian's commissioning from this same Aviation Officer Candidate School. He was ranked at the top of his class. It was a wonderful occasion and one of many highlights of our lives. As an aside, I was the first AOC pilot graduate to reach flag rank.

---

* Richard M. Nixon served as President of the United States from 20 January 1969 until his resignation on 9 August 1974.

Paul Stillwell: How would you describe your own feelings of patriotism in that growing-up period before you got into the Navy?

Admiral Osborn: Very much, because of my brother. I felt I was a real patriot. Another trait that has always been strong is the question of integrity. Integrity to me is the ultimate. If something comes down to whether you do it or you don't, how you deal with it, integrity has always been my standard. There have never been any shades of right and wrong. Maybe sometimes it has weighed too much or spilled over into the issue of compromise. You have to have compromise. In nearly every issue of importance there has to be a degree of compromise. I have always had trouble with that, and it probably cost me over the years. But whenever there was a decision with respect to right and wrong, there was never a question in my mind. But this Clinton thing—I have never been more upset in my life over the way this impeachment process has resolved, the way it was handled in Congress.* To have a President who lies under oath is far beyond the limits.

Paul Stillwell: On the radio yesterday I heard a pool of historians rating the 41 Presidents in terms of moral character and Clinton came in 41st.

Admiral Osborn: You know, every President has manipulated the facts at one time or another, to pull off what he wanted to do, or to cover the facts of an issue. Roosevelt lied about the Lend-Lease program and other issues that thrust us into World War II.† He manipulated the truth in order to make things happen the way he thought was right for the country.

Paul Stillwell: Politicians tell people what they think they want to hear.

---

* Bill Clinton served as President of the United States from 20 January 1993 to 20 January 2001. In 1998 the House of Representatives voted to impeach him on a number of grounds. When the impeachment was tried the following year the Senate could not muster sufficient votes to remove Clinton from office.
† Franklin D. Roosevelt served as President of the United States from 4 March 1933 until his death on 12 April 1945. The Lend-Lease Act, passed by the U.S. Congress on 11 March 1941, was a device that enabled the United States to provide military aid to Great Britain without intervening directly in the European war then in progress. The program was later expanded to include aid to other Allied nations as well.

Admiral Osborn: Yes, some of the things that Roosevelt did were not exactly honest with the electorate, but they probably were the right things to do under the circumstances. How do you decide that? Of course, that is totally different from Clinton. Clinton has a major character flaw.

Paul Stillwell: You mentioned the initials DOR. Lou Gossett mentioned DOR over and over. He was trying to force people to drop out, whereas your DI was trying to force you to stay in—an interesting contrast.

Admiral Osborn: All the way through, we had a feeling that these guys were trying to get us to quit; they were trying to find our breaking point. I think they pretty well know which ones are going to make it in the first place and which ones are worth keeping.

Paul Stillwell: So it's a useful weeding out.

Admiral Osborn: I have never been involved in the training command decision process, but I expect for every class that starts, the DIs have a pretty good feel for how many people the Navy wants to keep out of that group. Certainly that is the case in the flight phase. Once you get started flying, the criteria for a "down" can vary, and the criteria for how many "downs" are acceptable can vary depending on the number of graduates needed at that particular time.* Obviously this is all within prudent limits regarding quality.

Paul Stillwell: Sometimes the system works to save a person from himself. He is not really adapted to flying and the instructors want to get him out of there before he kills himself.

Please proceed to the next step, which was learning to fly.

---

* A "down" was an unsatisfactory grade given by an instructor pilot during a check flight.

Admiral Osborn: I enjoyed it, and I was good at it; didn't have any problems at all. I was a bit lucky, because on two occasions I was able to avoid "downs" that should have come. Maybe I didn't have as much integrity as I claimed [laughter]. Both occasions require some background information. During that period the training command was introducing new planes, the T-34 basic trainer and T-28 intermediate trainer, coincident with a slow phasing out of the SNJ.* Consequently, there was considerable shuffling of the training flow sequence. North Whiting had SNJs and South Whiting had T-34s. I did my first flying and solo work in the T-34, then went to Corry Field for instruments in the T-28.† The T-28 was a very high-powered training plane and it, like the T-34, had automatic fuel feed. We then went to Saufley Field for formation.‡

One day while we were at Saufley I came back into the landing pattern and forgot to drop my landing gear. Fortunately, as I was rolling in to final, one of the guys behind me saw it and hollered over the radio. I dropped the gear and went on in to land. The instructor didn't catch what happened, so I escaped unscathed.

The second incident was during gunnery training. Normally we would have done gunnery in the T-28 right there at Saufley, but the T-28 had developed G-force stress cracks. So they sent us to Barin Field and checked us out in the SNJ.§ The SNJ, first of all, was a tail-wheel plane. We had been flying tricycle landing gear up till that time. Also, the SNJ had two fuel tanks which had to be manually selected. During the course of the training I was on a triple-period gunnery hop out over the Gulf of Mexico. The instructor was towing the gunnery target sleeve. Four of us were above and behind the sleeve in formation. When it came your turn, you would peel off and make a diving gunnery run on the sleeve and return to the formation for another run. Just as I was

---

* The T-34 Mentor was a training aircraft manufactured by Beech. The Navy placed its first order in June 1954, a few months after the Air Force had adopted the plane for primary flight training. In 1952 the Navy had begun using North American's T-28 Trojan in its curriculum for pilots after a decision to standardize training techniques and equipment with the Air Force. The SNJ Texan was a training aircraft manufactured by North American Aviation. The Navy first ordered a version of the airplane in late 1936; the Army designation was AT-6. Versions of the Texan continued in use for Navy training well into the 1950s.
† Corry Field is part of the Pensacola Naval Air Station; it was named in honor of Lieutenant Commander William M. Corry, USN, naval aviator number 23.
‡ Saufley Field is part of the Pensacola Naval Air Station; it was named in honor of Lieutenant (junior grade) Richard C. Saufley, USN, naval aviator number 14.
§ Barin Field was part of the naval auxiliary air station at Foley, Alabama; it was named in honor of Lieutenant Louis T. Barin, USN, naval aviator number 56.

preparing to peel off for my run, with two others on my wing, my fuel tank ran dry and the engine abruptly quit. I had forgotten to switch tanks. I was hanging in the sky rapidly approaching stall speed, totally panicked, because all I could see was water below.

Eventually I managed to get the engine started, but in the interim my two wing mates, attempting to maintain position, had reached stall speed and spun out. The instructor was screaming at me to get moving. He was a screamer anyway. I finally made the run, and we finished up the flight. Back on the ground, my fellow students were not happy with me, but the instructor didn't find out what happened. Thus I escaped two sure "downs" and whatever negative fallout they would have triggered.

Paul Stillwell: Please talk to me about the initial stages of flying, learning to fly and moving on to solo.

Admiral Osborn: My first instructor at Whiting was a Marine by the name of John Hudson, who later became a three-star general.[*] He was a good instructor. Remembering that I got airsick on my only previous flight some five months before in Denver, all I was thinking about before the first flight at Whiting was whether there was going to be a repeat. We took off in the T-34, and I immediately had my head in the bag. He stuck with me, and I got through the rest of the flight. The same thing happened the next day, but I eventually got over the idea of airsickness and was judged safe for solo. Those first flights and the solo were a real thrill.

Paul Stillwell: Did you sense a feeling of exhilaration in the air?

Admiral Osborn: Yes, I felt it most at Saufley Field flying formation. I loved formation—the precision of moving in and maintaining position on the next airplane. I also enjoyed acrobatics. They teach you spin recovery, the loop, wingover, etc. The reason they teach these maneuvers is so you can recover if you ever get into uncontrolled

---

[*] He was Lieutenant Colonel John S. Hudson, USMC, at the time of the flight training.

flight. Once I got past the first couple of flights and the solo stage, I loved it all. From then on, until the end of my Navy flying, I always looked forward to the next flight.

Paul Stillwell: How capable were your instructors?

Admiral Osborn: I never had what I would consider a bad instructor. One Marine major at Corry Field was infamous as a screamer who gave a lot of "downs." From the time you first encountered him at the pre-flight brief until the flight was over, he screamed or berated all the time. As luck would have it, I drew him for my check flight for that stage of training. He made you feel like an idiot the entire flight. I was determined to get past him and did. A lot didn't. He was not a good instructor, in my view. The rest of my instructors were good. Most had a lot of experience, including some with World War II combat experience.

Paul Stillwell: Did you pick up the swagger that goes with being a naval aviator?

Admiral Osborn: A little bit. I wanted, in the worst way, to be an attack pilot in the AD Skyraider.* I was in that pipeline at Barin Field in the classroom preparing for field carrier landing practice (FCLP) in preparation for qualifying on board the training carrier. An administrative officer came in one day and said, "I've got a list here of your class. I'm going to read off every fourth name, and you are to detach immediately and report to Hutchison, Kansas, for multi-engine training." My name was called. I had great flight grades. That was a real disappointment. Those AD pilots ended up flying the A-4 in Vietnam with the highest casualties of the war.† Who knows what would have happened, but that is what I wanted to do. However, while at Hutchinson I met my wife!

Paul Stillwell: Please tell me about Hutchinson, Kansas.

---

* The Douglas AD Skyraider propeller-driven attack planes first entered fleet squadrons in late 1946. The AD-2 version was 38 feet long, wingspan of 50 feet, gross weight of 18,263 pounds, and top speed of 321 miles per hour. In September 1962 Skyraiders still in service were redesignated A-1s.
† The Douglas A4D Skyhawk attack plane first entered the fleet in October 1956 in squadron VA-72. The A4D was 40 feet, 4 inches long, wingspan of 27 feet, 6 inches, gross weight of 24,500 pounds, and top speed of 670 miles per hour. In 1962 the aircraft was redesignated the A-4.

Admiral Osborn: A godforsaken place. It wasn't all that different from where I grew up, but it seemed worse because the wind and the dust blew all the time. It is about 30 or 40 miles west of Topeka, out in the middle of farm country. We started out in the twin-engine Beechcraft SNB for instrument flight and then went to the P2V-3, where we soloed, and then went into the P2V-4.[*] Soloing the P2V-3 was interesting, because it was a monster airplane compared to what we had been flying.[†] It was very stiff on the controls and not very responsive. Those were very old airplanes. While I was there, the last P2V-3 retired. They were replaced by S2Fs.

Navigation was a significant part of the training. We learned to identify all the stars and used a bubble sextant which hung from an astrodome (bubble in the top of the plane) and required very accurate star identification. The idea was to look out of the astrodome, select three bright stars that were at approximately 120-degree angles, compute the data out of the manual, then shoot the stars. Later aircraft used a firmly mounted sextant which allowed presetting azimuth and elevation of a selected star so that star identification was nearly automatic. During early stages of the training we would go out at night, on the ground, and practice shooting the stars. This was wintertime in Kansas. It wasn't a lot of fun.

One incident stands out from the Hutchinson training. During a latter stage we flew a three-leg flight from Hutchinson to a beacon in New Mexico, then to a beacon in Texas, then back to Hutchinson. The three navigator trainees each took a leg to navigate. Each of us also flew copilot for one leg. I was the copilot for the first leg. As we made our turn over the New Mexico beacon in total darkness, the instructor pilot and I simultaneously saw the lights of a plane directly ahead of us. The pilot jerked the controls as hard as he could, and we missed the plane by a very few feet. I had a few

---

[*] The SNB Kansan was a training aircraft manufactured by Beech Aircraft Company. The Navy first ordered a version of the airplane in 1941; the Army designation of the equivalent plane was AT-11. When DoD introduced its unified designation system in 1962, SNBs still in use became either TC-45Js or RC-45Js.

[†] The Lockheed P2V Neptune was a land-based patrol plane that first entered an operational squadron in March 1947 in VP-ML-2. The P2V-3 was 77 feet, 10 inches long; wingspan of 100 feet; gross weight of 64,100 pounds, and top speed of 337 miles per hour. In 1962 the aircraft was redesignated the P-2.

close shaves in the air over the years, but that was the closest. We were on a visual flight rule (VFR) flight plan, meaning that we flew at an even 1,000-foot altitude, plus 500, or odd plus 500, depending on your heading. One of the planes was still at his previous leg's altitude. Thus the near miss.

Paul Stillwell: How did your future wife happen to be around Hutchinson, Kansas, at that time? Had she moved there from Nebraska?

Admiral Osborn: She wasn't at Hutchinson. I went home to Nebraska for the weekend. My sister-in-law's friend set me and one of my buddies up with blind dates. She was my blind date. She had a sister, so we took the two sisters out. Before we went to the door to pick them up, we flipped a coin to see who took whom. I frequently remind my wife that she either won or lost the flip.

Paul Stillwell: Did you after a time reconcile yourself to the patrol community?

Admiral Osborn: Yes, I did. There wasn't much choice. I've never been sorry about what happened, because it turned out very well for me.

Paul Stillwell: How much knowledge did you have of the Navy as a whole and where your piece fit into it?

Admiral Osborn: Not very much. We didn't get a lot of schooling on that kind of thing. We didn't get much on what the Navy looked like, or its structure, or any naval history to speak of. That is one of the reasons why the Naval Academy is so important. Those officers have that kind of knowledge. We didn't. We got four months; they get four years. That is a real difference. We were not ready to be true naval officers. It was very much learning by experience.

Paul Stillwell: You get so focused on your job that it precludes a broader picture.

Admiral Osborn: Yes, I read the Proceedings during the first years, the All Hands, Navy Times. Those three gave me what little bit of the big picture I knew. At the time of my first four-year tour, the Navy policy was to not show officers their fitness reports, unless it was adverse (the lowest ranking). Unless you had a CO who was a really good leader, you had very little firm indication of how you were performing.[*] A lot of skippers at that time did no counseling of their officers. They just couldn't bring themselves to tell an officer what his faults were. They also weren't used to praising people. Some of the great leaders you have interviewed never did any of that. Their long-term contribution to the Navy was fantastic, but there are some very famous senior officers who never took the time to counsel officers on their performance. It is a hard thing to do and a lot never quite get around to it. Certainly that has changed dramatically. Today counseling at fitness report time is required. The point is, that facet of leadership is part of officer education today, whether the officer is Naval Academy, OCS, or NROTC.[†]

Paul Stillwell: My recollection is that it was during the Admiral Zumwalt era as CNO that officers got much greater access to fitness reports than previously.

Admiral Osborn: There are two sides to that issue. I see some bad sides to what has happened with fitness reports. I am saying this from my active duty experience. I think it has gotten to the point that officers are so tuned to what their fitness report says that it steers the way they deal with everyday issues and how they conduct themselves as officers. I believe that the ranking system, where the individuals rank, has put us in a position where young officers really aren't themselves sometimes. They worry too much about where they stand fitness report wise and where their next duty station is going to be. At the time of my first tour, 1957-61, you didn't have the foggiest idea what your fitness report said, and you didn't worry about where you were going. You waited for the bureau to tell you where you were going next. Neither one of those were right, but the pendulum has swung too far the other way. As far as the structure of fitness reports, I

---

[*] CO—commanding officer.
[†] NROTC—Naval Reserve Officers' Training Corps.

worked on the structure of the fitness report form when I was in NMPC and used fitness reports constantly to make decisions about officer detailing.*

In my view, Admiral Boorda's fitness reporting system change was not a good one.† He was trying to get away from two or three or four competing officers in the same command being ranked number one. Even though there was a lot of that in the old system, you could still tell pretty well where that officer stood in relation to his peers. When you went into the tank as a selection board member, there was plenty of information to differentiate and pick the officer you wanted to select. Under the Boorda change, you can have two competing officers who are absolute superstars, but one has to be ranked number one, and one has to be ranked number two. There are situations where that is grossly unfair to one of the officers because he automatically falls out of contention for later command or choice assignment. Also, if these two are equally capable and one is a minority, the minority will get the nod for number one nine times out of ten.

There is another aspect of performance that I want to mention. We don't have enough risk takers in today's military. That is brought on by the intense competition for very limited choice assignments. Officers quickly learn that they had better fit into a fairly narrow range of performance criteria. In wartime situations, the prudent risk takers will be the most successful leaders. You cannot be afraid to take a chance in combat environment.

Paul Stillwell: I interrupted you before when you started to tell me about how the smart ones learn more about the Navy to get beyond their own job.

Admiral Osborn: The ones who really want to get the big picture take it upon themselves to learn. The other thing that we had at that time was a correspondence course program. There was a leadership correspondence course. I hated them and really didn't apply myself. But we had to do them. That may be why they did away with them. It was like

---

* NMPC—Naval Military Personnel Command, a title used for a time in the 1980s. Before and afterward, the organization has gone by the title Bureau of Naval Personnel.
† Admiral Jeremy M. Boorda, USN, served as Chief of Naval Operations from 23 April 1994 to 16 May 1996. As a vice admiral, he had been Chief of Naval Personnel from 9 August 1988 to 6 November 1991.

taking medicine for most naval officers. That was one way a "four-month wonder" learned something about the Navy.

Paul Stillwell: As you went through these various stages of aviation training pipeline, did you have a growing sense of confidence?

Admiral Osborn: I don't know that I had a growing sense of confidence at that time. I think that began to come after I reported into my first squadron and started flying. I received orders to Patrol Squadron 17 in Whidbey Island, Washington. I arrived there shortly before we were due to deploy to Iwakuni, Japan, and was assigned to the flight crew of a P2V Neptune patrol plane as the lead navigator. We went to Japan for a six-month deployment. I was navigating for a plane commander with the philosophy that if you are the navigator you are going to navigate, and you don't get any time in the front end. I navigated that entire deployment, stuck in the back of the plane. It was very frustrating; nevertheless, that is the way it turned out. On the other hand, my plane commander was a very fatherly guy who took me under his wing. He treated me pretty well and gave me a lot of tips on life and squadron kind of things.

Paul Stilwell: Who was he?

Admiral Osborn: His name was Jim Clampet.* He was an old hand; he'd been in the Navy about 15 years. He was kind of a permanent full lieutenant. These were people who had come in during World War II, and promotions were pretty much nonexistent. Some of them were serving out their time to retirement.

At any rate, we deployed to Japan, and it was quite a memorable experience. We arrived and were sent on detachment to Chitose Air Force Base on the northern island of Hokkaido, where we flew missions in the Sea of Japan off the coast of the Soviet Union. At the end of about two weeks we were ordered back to Iwakuni, which was our deployment base. We had another crew with us that had a couple of daredevil pilots. They departed Chitose to return to Iwakuni. They took off about 0530 and made a low

---

* Lieutenant James V. Clampet, USN; he made lieutenant commander in 1959.

pass over the base at about 50 feet, shook the building we were sleeping in, and went on their way.

So, the next morning we were leaving, and my plane commander decided he would do the same thing. It happened to be a Sunday morning. We took off, and he requested a low pass from the tower. Unfortunately, the base commander, an Air Force colonel, was already upset about the previous morning's event. So when we literally shook the base on Sunday morning while he was sleeping, it was the straw that broke the camel's back. We went on our way, did our mission en route, and landed at Iwakuni. Backtracking slightly, when we had made the low pass, unbeknownst to my plane commander, I got the Very pistol (flare pistol) out. As we were going down the runway on a high-speed, 50-foot pass, I fired a couple of flares out of the plane just to add a little spark to the whole thing.

When we landed in Iwakuni there was a large entourage waiting to welcome us, including the wing commander, squadron commanding officer, and executive officer. It wasn't a friendly welcome. I wasn't privy to the conversations that took place in the captain's office. All the sudden, the plane commander came out, got the copilot and myself together, and said, "They're talking about somebody shooting flares on the runway. Do either of you know what they are talking about?" Of course, I had to come clean. Not only was my plane commander in deep kimchee, I wasn't in very good shape myself for a while.* [Laughter]

Paul Stillwell: What were the consequences of the deep kimchee?

Admiral Osborn: It looked for a while like both the plane commanders were going to be grounded and lose their plane commander designations. The air-traffic-control people in Tokyo got involved in it, so it got very sticky. It wasn't a very good thing for our commanding officer obviously. He wasn't the type of guy who was going to take the fall by himself. Eventually they decided not to ground these two guys. It didn't affect me any at all, although that commanding officer, for the time he was there, gave me an eye-opening fitness report. The old report form had a block on the far right entitled

---

* In this context "kimchee" may be taken as a Korean synonym for manure.

"adverse." He marked me in every category in the next-to-last block adjacent to the adverse block. The marks were conspicuously placed over on the right-hand side of that next-to-last block. Of course, I didn't know this, because in those days you didn't see your fitness reports unless you went to the Bureau of Naval Personnel in D.C. to a fitrep reviewing room.* Several years later I was in Washington and looked at my reports with dismay.

The interesting thing was that I was the assistant weight and balance officer at the time—kind of a job on paper that didn't amount to much. I don't think the flare incident was the reason for those marks, but I never could figure out what caused such low marks, and no one else could tell me either. I asked a number of people later, "Was I really that bad?"

They said, "No, we thought you were doing all right."

I'd like to digress for a moment and relate an interesting story about Chitose Air Force Base. Chitose had been a Japanese Army base during World War II. Upon U.S. occupation, the U.S. Air Force stationed fighter planes there. When we arrived, they were flying F-86s, very modern fighters.† During the two weeks we were there, the scheduled return of the base to the Japanese Government took place. Literally overnight the star was painted off and the rising sun painted on all the aircraft. U.S. Air Force pilots left, and the Japanese pilots took over the fighter squadrons. It all went very smoothly.

Paul Stillwell: What else do you have to say about the leadership qualities of your first skipper?

Admiral Osborn: He was a transport pilot, and I don't say that in a derogative manner; that was his background. He had a lot of flight hours, like 8,000 or 10,000. This was a guy who flew transports through the war. He was just not a very good skipper. He was a

---

* The Arlington Annex is a large, multi-wing building near the Pentagon and the Arlington National Cemetery. It contains the headquarters of the Marine Corps and for many years had the Bureau of Naval Personnel also.
† The F-86 Sabre jet, built by North American, was a swept-wing Air Force fighter that achieved combat success in the Korean War. The Navy counterpart was the FJ-2 Fury.

questionable pilot too. He led us on some formation-mining missions during which he did some things that were absolutely unsafe and put the whole flight in jeopardy. He was not a very nice guy, and he didn't lead very well. I don't remember of him ever complimenting anyone, and he was very harsh with people. He didn't provide a very good leadership example in Japan either. Almost as soon as he arrived he was out in town finding a Japanese honey to sleep with. He spent every night in town rather than his BOQ room.* I don't know if there was a connection, but we probably had 25 or 30 officers who did the same thing throughout the deployment. For a Nebraska farm boy it was quite a shock because we were very strong church-going people. I just couldn't imagine someone living this way.

Paul Stillwell: Was that useful to you in showing you some things to avoid when you became more senior?

Admiral Osborn: I think so, yes. You watch and observe. I had another CO in that same squadron, Richard Larson, who was one of my better COs, but he had a bad habit of screaming.† When he got upset he would go into outrageous theatrics and screaming. He simply lost his composure when he got upset. In the long run, he was a very good CO. He supported his good people and was very hard on the ones who weren't so good. He was probably a little too harsh on some, but I still considered him a good leader. His son is a Naval Academy graduate and was commanding officer of a squadron at one time.‡

The previous CO I had in VP-17 was John Wheatley.§ He was test pilot and also a transport pilot. He had flown the Berlin Airlift and all over Alaska, so he understood the unique flying conditions which prevail in Alaska.** Alaska is one of the worst places in the world to fly. It was even worse then, because in those days the weather forecasting business was very imprecise. The weather systems coming out of Siberia were very

---
* BOQ—bachelor officers' quarters.
† Commander Richard Larson, USN, commanded Patrol Squadron 17 from April 1959 to April 1960.
‡ His son, Robin C. Larson, USN, graduated from the Naval Academy in the class of 1967.
§ Commander John P. Wheatley, USN, commanded Patrol Squadron 17 from April 1958 to April 1959.
** On 1 April 1948 the Soviet Union began a land blockade of the Allied sectors of Berlin, preventing overland transport from West Germany. U.S. and British airplanes then began and airlift that flew food and coal into the city until the blockade was lifted on 30 September 1949.

unpredictable and, also, we didn't have any weather observation stations in Siberia, so we didn't know what was coming. You constantly found yourself in flying conditions that weren't predicted. Many times you would have 100-mile-per-hour winds at 6,000 feet mauling you around.

The only navigation aids on airways at that time were what they called "radio range." To fly from Point A to Point B on an airway chart you would fly by listening for a Morse code "A" or "N" or neither (a null). If you were to the left of the centerline of the airway you would hear an "A;" if to the right, an "N;" if on line, a null. That is the way you navigated from one airway radio range station to another. Arriving at your destination station, it was not easy to fly an instrument approach to landing with 100-mile-per-hour winds. It was very difficult even with low winds to stay right on the beam.

In the months prior to my second deployment, Commander Wheatley flew with a number of squadron pilots and began to realize we were not prepared for Alaska. He, therefore, personally embarked on a training program in Link trainers affectionately known as "idiot boxes," which were generic cockpits fed by an analog computer to simulate three dimensional flight in instrument weather conditions.[*] If you can fly instruments in an idiot box, you can fly them in a plane, because they were very sensitive and erratic to control. He kept us in those trainers for hours. When we went to Alaska for that deployment we were prepared for those weather conditions. If he hadn't done that, we would have been in serious trouble. This was a little bit different form of leadership, but he had the sense to teach us skills and preparation.

I cannot overstate the effect weather has on operations in Alaska and the Aleutians. One of the key players in the Aleutians during the war was Commander James Russell, the CO of one of the PBY squadrons.[†] During our deployment, he visited Kodiak as a retired admiral and spoke to our wardroom about his World War II experiences. It was fascinating. The Thousand Mile War by Brian Garfield graphically

---
[*] The Link trainers were aircraft simulators manufactured by the Link Company.
[†] Commander James S. Russell, USN, commanded Patrol Squadron 42 from July 1941 to October 1942. The squadron was flying the PBY Catalina, the principal patrol plane used by the U.S. Naval during World War II. The oral history of Russell, who eventually retired as a four-star admiral, is in the Naval Institute collection.

describes World War II action in the Aleutians, and the role weather played in the battles.* Commander Russell is mentioned several times in the book.

Another key player in the Aleutians during the war was Robert C. Reeve, who later formed Reeve Aleutian Airline. His planes served Adak during my deployments there.† Early on, they were mostly four-engine Douglas transports. Some did not have reversible propellers. On one occasion at Adak I observed a Reeve plane land on ice with a combination tail and cross wind. In order to stop before the end of the runway, the pilot applied maximum power to two engines on one side and was able to cartwheel the plane 180 degrees and stay on the runway. I was told this happened many times.

Paul Stillwell: I have heard examples of the camaraderie that existed in carrier squadrons as they lived together in the ready room and shipboard life. What is the comparable situation in a patrol squadron?

Admiral Osborn: Its not quite as close, but still on deployment the officers are all living together in the BOQ, so there is tremendous camaraderie there in getting to know each other and working together. Then in a patrol squadron flight crew there is a microcosm of a team. That was where I first began to understand what leadership and teamwork were all about—instilling a sense of teamwork in your people. Because I was a pretty good pilot, I was given a flight crew earlier than most. In fact, I was John Coughlin's copilot when we got ready to go to Alaska on deployment.‡ The skipper decided to make John the officer-in-charge of our Adak detachment.

About three weeks before deployment I got John Coughlin's flight crew. I was by far the junior plane commander in the squadron. The crew I took over was very young. Learning how to deal with those officers and enlisted men, get the most out of them, and fly the plane safely was where I really began to understand how much influence you can have over other people. I learned what power you have over people if you do the right

---

* Brian Garfield, <u>The Thousand-Mile War: World War II in Alaska and the Aleutians</u> (Garden City, New York: Doubleday, 1969).
† Adak, Alaska, is the site of a U.S. naval facility in the Aleutian Islands chain.
‡ Lieutenant John T. Coughlin, USN. The oral history of Coughlin, who retired as a rear admiral, is in the Naval Institute collection.

kinds of things and treat them right and guide them; criticize them if they need it, and in private; compliment them if they do good, in public.

Paul Stillwell: Can you just run through the different spots in a patrol plane crew, please.

Admiral Osborn: A patrol plane commander, a copilot, two navigators. At that time there was a radio operator, a radar operator, electronic countermeasures (ECM) operator, an ordnanceman, a plane captain and a second plane captain. The plane captain was very important because he preflighted the plane, he was the mechanic, he understood the engines, and he was the enlisted leader of the crew. That crew composition has changed with the advent of the P-3.* My plane captain had just received his qualification. As a second class petty officer he was the titular leader of the enlisted crew, even though we had a chief petty officer as radio operator. The reason the chief wasn't the crew leader was because he couldn't lead. This created its own undercurrent. It was not well received by the chief, but there was no way that chief was going to be the guy that kept the enlisted men heading in the same direction. It took a little ingenuity to make that work.

Paul Stillwell: Please describe the P2V as an aircraft and as to mission fulfillment.

Admiral Osborn: The P2V had two reciprocating engines and two jet engines. The jet engines were used to gain additional thrust for takeoff and also for high-speed, low-altitude mining runs. If you ever lost a reciprocating engine in flight, you could use one of the jets to assist. However, the jets were very inefficient with respect to fuel consumption. The airplane was used for antisubmarine (ASW) and reconnaissance patrols primarily. Most of our work was reconnaissance along the Russian coastline in the Bering Sea and Sea of Japan. We had ECM, and we did have ASW capability, but it was pretty rudimentary. Our ability to detect and track a submarine was pretty limited,

---

* The Lockheed P-3 Orion (originally P3V) is a high-performance land-based patrol plane. It first entered operational squadrons in August 1962. The P-3C is 116 feet, 10 inches long; wingspan of 99 feet, 8 inches; gross weight of 135,000 pounds, and top speed of 473 miles per hour.

although we didn't think of it that way at the time. We had a magnetic anomaly detector (MAD) in the tail of the airplane so that when you did get the submarine localized down to a small area, if you could gain MAD contact, you had a precise position to attack with a torpedo. We carried torpedoes and depth bombs, depending on the situation.

Paul Stilwell: Were sonobuoys your primary detection source?

Admiral Osborn: Yes. At that time the process was quite imprecise. We placed a sonobuoy at the most likely position of the submarine with four additional sonobuoys in a circle at 90-degree positions surrounding the estimated datum.* You could select with a switch which sonobuoy you wanted to listen to with headphones. By comparing relative intensity of the noise from sonobuoys with contact, you would scribe arcs on a plotting sheet to gain an intersection of most probable location of the target. It was very difficult to pinpoint the submarine by this method because the sub was always moving. Later on, while I was in that squadron, we gained some equipment called "Julie/Jezebel."† By placing two sonobuoys in a line about 2,000 yards apart adjacent to the sub's suspected position and "bombing" one buoy with a practice depth charge, an echo range was attained. That gave more capability, but it was still pretty rudimentary by today's standards.

Paul Stillwell: Did there come a point where you had a visual display from the sonobuoys?

Admiral Osborn: No, that came later. Jezebel offered a paper display of the submarine's frequency "signature." It was introduced as I was leaving the squadron and wasn't being used, because it was not very effective at that point. Rarely could you distinguish between a submarine and a surface unit. Later, that concept became the system that is used today in a more refined form.

---

* Datum is the last known or estimated position of the target submarine.
† Julie was a type of submarine detection system in which a small depth charge produced a sonic pulse that could be received by passive sonobuoys. It was replaced by a passive low-frequency system known as Jezebel or LOFAR, low-frequency acquisition and ranging.

Paul Stillwell: What was involved in your mining work?

Admiral Osborn: When I joined the squadron, the title of the squadron was VAHM-10, Attack Mining Squadron Ten. The mission was mining, not ASW. We had special aircraft that were designated P2V-6M; the "M" stood for mining. The mission was to place mines in harbors. When I got my orders at Hutchison, Kansas, they told me I was going to be flying A3D Skywarrior mining jets.* Somewhere between the time I left the training command and arrived at the squadron, that was shelved so we never got A3Ds. So we were a mining squadron, and they then changed us from mining to ASW and gave us different P2 aircraft, but we still had mining as a secondary mission. We did a lot of mining training. We would take off from Whidbey Island, Washington, and fly all the way to San Diego to a mining range off the coast.

Paul Stillwell: How much precision were you able to achieve?

Admiral Osborn: Not very much, because we didn't have very precise navigation. You really did it almost totally by line of sight from planned visual references. A beacon in the area would help precision, but that was not very realistic for a wartime situation. Operations were mostly daytime.

Paul Stillwell: What more can you say about those intelligence flights off the Soviet Union?

Admiral Osborn: We were primarily conducting Soviet ship surveillance. We flew low-altitude rigging passes on merchantmen, looking for military cargo. We also observed Soviet fleet operations and recorded ECM data. We did not normally carry Russian linguists. We were required to stay 30 miles off the Soviet coastline. If you

---

* The Douglas A3D Skywarrior first entered fleet squadrons in 1956 as a carrier-based heavy bomber. It was reclassified as the A-3 in 1962. The A3D-2 version was 76 feet long; wingspan of 72 feet; gross weight of 82,000 pounds; and top speed of 610 miles per hour. It had a maximum bomb capacity of 12,000 pounds.

strayed across the 30-mile line, that was a big deal. We had a warning system to tell us when we were in danger.

Paul Stillwell: What sort of a warning system?

Admiral Osborn: I will only say that there was a system to warn us if we had strayed, or if we were in possible danger.

Paul Stillwell: During the Cold War some U.S. patrol planes were shot down. Was that ever a concern?

Admiral Osborn: Yes, it was a great concern. We were intercepted by Soviet aircraft three or four times during that deployment. Two MiGs would make the intercept.[*] One would remain high and behind us while the other made a close pass on our aircraft. The year before, a patrol plane had been shot down in the Sea of Japan. Two or three years previous to that a patrol plane was severely damaged by fire from a MiG in the Bering Strait area and crash landed on St. Lawrence Island in the Bering Sea. Just before our deployment, a VQ-1 P4M Mercator based at Iwakuni was badly damaged by MiG fire but was able to limp into a Japanese civil airport at Miho.[†] Some crew members were killed by the strafing.

We wore rubber water survival suits, affectionately known as "poopy suits," which completely covered the body up to the neck. The suit "sealed" around the neck by virtue of a tight rubber ring. It was impossible to function through a flight with that rubber nearly choking you, so we had a metal ring which just fit over your head to hold the rubber ring off your neck during normal operations. Over time the suits developed cracks and leaks, and the rubber neck ring stretched. All this rendered the suits a hazard rather that a help, because water would have immediately seeped into the suits in actual emergency conditions. Actually the suits were a psychological tool only, because if you

---

[*] MiG is the designation of a number of Soviet fighter planes that originated in the Mikoyan-Gurevich design bureau.
[†] On 16 June 1959 two MiG fighters attacked and damaged a P4M reconnaissance plane during a mission over international waters off the coast of Korea.

ever had to enter the icy waters of that area, you would only survive a few minutes with a perfect suit. We hated those suits because you constantly perspired and were soaking wet when you took them off.

Paul Stillwell: How much stamina did those patrols take?

Admiral Osborn: We could fly about ten hours. They were tiring because we were under a degree of stress most of the time.

Paul Stillwell: Are there any interesting things you remember on these surveillance flights?

Admiral Osborn: The most interesting was flying out of Adak, Alaska. During one period of time we would get an order to launch, go to a certain area about halfway between the Aleutians and Midway Island, and look at everything in that area. If we found anything unusual we were to report it immediately. That is all they told us. One morning we went to the assigned area, descended through the clouds, and there we saw three large Soviet ships with huge bubbles on the decks. They were the oddest-looking ships we had ever seen. We reported them, and they turned out to be the Soviet missile range instrumentation ships that were positioned at the splashdown point for their long-range missile tests. They recorded telemetrically pertinent missile data and recovered the test capsules. This is the first time they had been located by U.S. surveillance. Higher authority had not told us what to look for or any other information about them. After that, we covered them whenever they were deployed to the mid-Pacific. A couple of times we were on station when the missile came in. We had electronics on board that would alert when a missile was coming in. Our job was to observe, particularly the splashdown.

We also flew ice reconnaissance flights out of Eielson Air Force Base at Fairbanks. We carried a trained meteorologist ice observer over the northern ice, sometimes almost to the pole. Navigation was difficult. Because of severe magnetic anomaly, we used grid navigation, which required great care and attention. Flight operations out of Eielson were challenging in 40-50-degree-below-zero weather.

Paul Stillwell: There was kind of a cat-and-mouse-game aspect to these Cold War operations.

Admiral Osborn: It was definitely a cat-and-mouse game. The flights along the Soviet coastline were very uncomfortable, because we never knew when they were going to come out, and, as you say, there had been quite a few U.S. planes shot down.

Paul Stillwell: What did you do in your off-duty periods in that squadron during the deployment?

Admiral Osborn: In Japan I did as much sightseeing as possible. I went to Hiroshima, which was only about 40 miles away.* That was in 1957, so it wasn't all that long after the atomic bomb had been dropped. It was a very unsettling experience because most of the damage still showed, and they had one little building where there were a number of pictures of destruction and radiated people. The Japanese people didn't like having us there. It was a memorable experience that made you do a lot of thinking. I went to town occasionally at night. The food was fantastic; I couldn't get enough of the food. I enjoyed Japan: the people, the culture, the scenery. It was a great experience. When we departed to come home, my wife back at Whidbey Island was very close to giving birth to our first child. We got as far as Kwajelein Island and lost an engine, so we spent ten days on that small island after a six-month deployment—not much fun knowing that my wife was about to deliver. Fortunately I got home in time.

Paul Stillwell: What can you say about the Whidbey Island area?

---

* In the first combat use of atomic bombs, U.S. B-29 bombers hit Hiroshima, on the island of Honshu, on 6 August 1945 and Nagasaki, on Kyushu, on 9 August.

Admiral Osborn: Whidbey Island is about 90 miles northwest of Seattle. Absolutely spectacular scenery, but for people stationed there, a very isolated spot. You either had to take the ferry to Seattle or drive north, reverse course, and go south quite a distance. It was sort of an isolated lifestyle and very much a rural, forested, and farming community. The town, Oak Harbor, was very small, so you were kind of off by yourself. It has grown up a lot since then. The Navy, in addition to P2s, had A3D Skywarriors, so it was a very busy air station.

Paul Stillwell: What do you remember about the atmosphere in Alaska when you were off duty?

Admiral Osborn: It was the O-club every night, because that was where we ate and gathered. I did some hunting. A lot of people fished. When the king salmon did their run up the river near the air station, they were so thick it was like you could walk across on them without getting wet. Amazing sight. The people that did fish used treble hooks and snagged the salmon in their back—a fish every cast.

At the end of my active duty requirement I had decided to get out of the Navy. As the day approached, I had checked out of the squadron and done everything except pick up my separation and travel checks, and check out with the duty officer the next day to become a civilian. The movers had already taken most of our household goods. At that point I was planning to fly for an airline but had not done much with regard to job search. That night I went home and told my wife that I wasn't feeling well and said, "I think I know why I'm not feeling good. I'm not sure we are doing the right thing". So we sat down and talked. The outcome was that I called up the skipper that night at home and asked if there was any possibility of coming back to work and staying in the Navy. He sent off a message to the Bureau of Naval Personnel and requested that my release from active duty be nullified. The next day I was back in the squadron.

Paul Stillwell: What year was that?

Admiral Osborn: That was 1960. I spent an additional year in VP-17 and then went to VP-31 at NAS North Island in Coronado, California.* VP-31 was a newly formed Pacific Fleet readiness training squadron. The squadron mission was aircraft-specific training of officers and aircrewmen to prepare them for duty in the fleet squadrons. That was then a new concept and is still in effect. I was sent there as a flight instructor. After I had been there a few months, the CO called me in and asked if I would be interested in being the squadron liaison to Commander Naval Air Force Pacific Fleet, the senior command to VP-31. I had gone to the squadron to fly airplanes so was not too interested. He persisted and said it was a great career opportunity. He said he had picked me because he considered me the best officer for the job. I would be working for a Navy captain and learning more about the big picture. He said I could still fly part time.

By that time I had gotten the message that this wasn't really a volunteer situation. I went to AirPac and worked for Captain Charlie Merryman, a wonderful old guy who was nearing the end of his career.† He was very powerful in that particular hierarchy. I was primarily helping with the introduction of the new P-3 aircraft to the Pacific Fleet. At that time there were two squadrons in the Atlantic Fleet. When it came time to form the first Pacific Fleet P-3 unit, I was one of the four pilots selected to form a detachment of VP-31 at Moffett Field near San Francisco.‡ So we four officers and 12 enlisted men moved into a totally empty airship hangar with no desks, no chairs, just walls. A very challenging task that called for a lot of innovation. At the time, Lockheed was at Moffett Field training the first fleet squadron, VP-46, to fly the plane. We received our training from Lockheed in VP-46 airplanes and then received our first plane. We immediately began an intensive flying schedule because we had the responsibility of training the second fleet squadron. The timeline was very tight.

Paul Stillwell: How did the P-3 differ from the P-2?

---

* North Island Naval Air Station is on the end of the Coronado peninsula, across the harbor from San Diego.
† Captain Charles A. Merryman, Jr., USN.
‡ Moffett Field Naval Air Station, Sunnyvale, California, was located ten miles north of San Jose, at the southern tip of San Francisco Bay. It was named in honor of Rear Admiral William A. Moffett, USN, first Chief of the Bureau of Aeronautics. Detachment Alfa of VP-31 was established on 4 January 1963.

Admiral Osborn: A totally different plane, larger, more maneuverable, easier to fly, hydraulic-assisted controls. A very versatile and capable plane. Four very powerful engines with immediate thrust response. More room inside for movement and electronics equipment. Much faster. You could go out 1,000 miles, operate for four or five hours on station, and return to base. The plane was designed to fly 10- to 11-hour patrols. The electronics equipment was new. It was fun to be involved because we were the envy of the fleet.

Captain Merryman told our skipper to plan a flight to WestPac to show off the plane to the patrol forces and the naval leadership in Seventh Fleet. Also, to consider flying a non-stop flight from the U.S. to Japan. At that time Lockheed had flown a P-3 from California to Paris, about 6,000 miles. That was with the direction of prevailing winds. Flying from California to Japan was strictly a headwind situation and problematical. I was one of the four pilots led by our CO. After extensive planning, we flew non-stop from Moffett Field to Atsugi Air Station near Tokyo. Not only a first, but has never been done since in a turboprop plane. It was a very tight set of parameters. When we landed we had about 15 minutes of fuel remaining. Our alternate was Misawa Air Force Base in northern Japan. We lost all radio communications about halfway across and didn't know that our alternate was below minimums. As we got near Japan, we were able to talk to another aircraft and learned that Atsugi's weather was bad; also, that Misawa was not suitable. We had no choice but to continue on to Atsugi, where we made it in just under minimums.

Paul Stillwell: When did that flight take place and did it achieve Captain Merryman's objectives?

Admiral Osborn: The flight was in the spring of 1963. I think it did do what he had in mind. Once we got to Atsugi, we went to Okinawa to the maritime base, then to Cubi in the Philippines, and on to Iwakuni, Japan. So we took the plane around and showed it to dignitaries, our maritime squadrons, and some Japanese officials. Eventually the Japanese acquired and built the P-3. That was probably part of the scheme. The plane performed beautifully on that trip. We flew over 60 hours and had only a couple of minor problems, which was remarkable. The P-3 has been a very reliable plane over the years but is getting old now and needs to be replaced, which is a current issue. The mission has evolved to new requirements. The plane is now doing overland reconnaissance along with its long-time missions. The antisubmarine mission has diminished in importance with the end of the Cold War. However, the ASW threat really hasn't gone away with the proliferation of countries now operating diesel submarines. The need for long-range reconnaissance capability is stronger than ever.

Paul Stillwell: There was a plan for a P-7. Has that gone away?

Admiral Osborn: Yes, that program succumbed to some severe budgetary problems. There is an ongoing program to develop a new long-range maritime patrol plane, but the program has not attained full definition.

Paul Stillwell: Did you, in effect, become a fleet replacement squadron since you were the first on the West Coast?

Admiral Osborn: At that time, VP-31 was doing P-2 training and P-5 seaplane training.[*] As more squadrons transitioned to the P-3, the parent squadron at North Island got smaller and the detachment at Moffett got larger. As the last squadrons transitioned to the P-3, all training was at Moffett and the North Island operation closed down. VP-31 ended up being a squadron of over 20 planes at Moffett. Years later, when Moffett Field closed, all P-3 replacement training went to Jacksonville.[†]

Paul Stillwell: What do you remember about the Moffett area as a place to have a young family?

---

[*] The Martin P5M Marlin was the U.S. Navy's last operational flying boat. It entered fleet service in 1948 and was last used in 1966. In 1962 it was redesignated P-5.
[†] Moffett Field was phased out as a naval air station because of the base realignment and closure process. Most of the station was transferred to the National Aeronautics and Space Administration on 1 July 1994 and renamed "Moffett Federal Airfield."

Admiral Osborn: We ended up with four tours at Moffett. It was a nice place to live—very expensive. When we first went there in 1963-64, Silicon Valley was nothing but prune orchards. Hewlett-Packard and Varian were really the only two major electronics firms in the area.

There is one other item that I would like to mention at this time. When I was on the AirPac staff I was first introduced to the parochialism that exists between TacAir and maritime air.* It is an unfortunate thing, a fact of life and will probably always be a fact of life, but it is not good for naval aviation. ComNavAirPac was primarily a carrier aviation staff. It was quite an eye-opener to find yourself in the position of a second cousin twice removed. You didn't get much respect.

Paul Stillwell: In what way did that manifest itself on that staff?

Admiral Osborn: Snide comments, and it was clear as you walked around the halls that they didn't consider you a first-rate pilot, and you were in a business that wasn't really needed. One of the things that nurtured it was the per diem issue.† When a VP squadron goes on deployment they get a fairly healthy per diem. When a TacAir squadron deploys they get nothing. The per diem was more than the cost of living, which meant extra cash in the pocket. This inequity still prevails, and it is not right. When I was Commander Patrol Wings Pacific I tried to get it revamped completely and basically done away with. My plan would have allowed deployed personnel to submit a claim for any extra expense. It went down in flames very quickly. Back to parochialism. It is alive and well but not quite as much as it used to be.

Paul Stillwell: Before World War II the practice was to rotate pilots among different types of aircraft, and then during the war and afterward that gave way to specialization.

---

* TacAir refers to tactical aircraft, essentially carrier-based fighters and attack planes; maritime air refers primarily to land-based patrol planes. VP is the shorthand designation generally used for the Navy's patrol aircraft.
† Per diem payments are made to personnel away from their home station to cover living expenses.

Admiral Osborn: My sense is that people like Admiral Tom Moorer, who started out in seaplanes, although I was never real close to him professionally, probably didn't have that attitude about patrol aviation.* It varies today. Some flag officers that were my peers looked at aviation matters and requirements in a broader, more objective manner.

Paul Stillwell: Was there a perception on the part of TacAir people that you had an easier life?

Admiral Osborn: Absolutely. I think that is the main sticker. Have you been in combat? No. Have you landed on a carrier? No. It is detrimental to the whole process. Helicopters fall in there somewhere. That is a bit curious, because helicopter flying is more demanding and dangerous sometimes that carrier operations. The helicopter guys on carriers get the same treatment as VP guys. It's just not quite as open.

Paul Stillwell: You had experienced a lot of personal growth then by the time you got up through that squadron at Moffett Field in terms of professionalism and experience.

Admiral Osborn: I had some unusual opportunities that helped in that regard: getting picked to fly the P-3, go to the AirPac staff, and having a key role in the Pacific Fleet P-3 introduction.

Paul Stillwell: Are you ready to go to ASW Group Five?

Admiral Osborn: When orders time came around at VP-31, the skipper called me in and said he had been queried by the bureau as to whether I would be interested in being an aide to an admiral.† I said, "No, I'm not interested at all and don't want anything to do with it. Just tell them no." He suggested that we think about it a little bit. Eventually I caved and ended up going to the staff of ASW Group Five in USS Bennington at Long

---

* Admiral Thomas H. Moorer, USN, served as Chief of Naval Operations from 1 August 1967 to 1 July 1970. His oral history is in the Naval Institute collection.
† This is a reference to the Bureau of Naval Personnel.

Beach.* The admiral at the time was Turner F. Caldwell.† Talk about someone making a contribution. He and Marine General Marion Carl were compatriots in the navy flight-testing program at Edwards where Carl set a new speed record.‡ Caldwell had set a record shortly before that.§ That plane hangs in the Air and Space Museum.

Admiral Caldwell was a very soft-spoken gentleman. He didn't look like a naval aviator at all—small, wrinkled. He was the first OP-095, the antisubmarine warfare directorate under the CNO. When Congress decided that they needed to do something about antisubmarine warfare he was the man that got the job. He was only Commander ASW Group Five for a few months because he was ordered to the Pentagon for that job on short notice. I probably wasn't much use to him as an aide, because I made a lot of mistakes in the early period, as most aides do. I joined the staff in Long Beach. We were getting ready to deploy to the Tonkin Gulf. Admiral Caldwell loved to hunt, so we would go out to Los Alamitos NAS and hunt doves.** He liked to sit and let the doves come to him. He told me many stories about his experiences. Trouble was, I didn't have any appreciation of who he was or what he had done until much later. He was very philosophical about his past.

Paul Stillwell: Please tell me about aide mistakes.

Admiral Osborn: Wearing the wrong uniform, forgetting the admiral's sword for a ceremony, I could go on and on!

---

* USS Bennington (CV-20) was originally commissioned 6 August 1944 as an attack carrier, decommissioned in 1946. In the early 1950s she was modernized and recommissioned in November 1952 as CVA-20. On 30 June 1959 she was reclassified as an antisubmarine warfare carrier (CVS-20). In that role she had the following characteristics: standard displacement: 33,100 tons; length, 899 feet; beam, 101 feet; maximum width, 192 feet; top speed, 33 knots.
† Rear Admiral Turner F. Caldwell, Jr., USN, became Commander Carrier Division 19 on 27 September 1963. In January 1964 the command was redesignated Anti-Submarine Warfare Group Five. Turner was detached in August 1964 and later that month became Director of Anti-Submarine Warfare Programs, Office of the Chief of Naval Operations.
‡ On 25 August 1947, Major Marion E. Carl, USMC, set a new world speed record of 650.796 miles per hour while flying a Douglas Skystreak D-558-1 over a three-kilometer course at Muroc, California.
§ On 20 August 1947, as a commander, Caldwell set a new world speed record of 640.663 miles per hour while flying a Douglas Skystreak D-558-1 over a three-kilometer course at Muroc, California.
** The former Los Alamitos Naval Air Station is about nine miles northeast of Long Beach, California. It closed as a naval air station in 1972 and is now an Army Airfield and reserve training facility.

Paul Stillwell: What is the role of an aide to an admiral?

Admiral Osborn: It varies with the individuals involved, of course. At that time, aide to an admiral flying his flag from a carrier was responsible for the admiral's barge, the band, the flag mess, the Marine orderlies and the admiral's schedule. There are those that would say it is a tougher job on a carrier than ashore. I wouldn't necessarily agree with that, because you run into more unusual circumstances ashore. In the carrier job you are the division officer for the barge crew and the band and the flag mess crew. The band presented a special challenge because the band members were civilians in naval uniforms. We had a black mess chief over Filipino mess stewards, which also presented a special challenge. You also stood a regular staff watch on the flag bridge, so it was a pretty busy day. I wanted to get qualified as an officer of the deck under way, so I stood both flag bridge watches and carrier bridge watches. This meant an hour or two nap two or three times a day, and that was it. You get used to it, sleeping anytime you get a chance.

Paul Stillwell: This was a whole different culture when you moved aboard a carrier.

Admiral Osborn: I'll say. Just finding my way around was a major task. I got lost trying to do something important. Backtracking a minute, Admiral Bob Macpherson had relieved Admiral Caldwell before we left Long Beach to go on deployment.* Macpherson was another soft-spoken personality. Fortunately I worked for admirals who were fairly easygoing and understanding and bent over backwards to overlook a few mistakes. As a junior officer aide you get to see and hear things that are very broadening. I would sit in on very sensitive conversations and be privy to very personal things. When the admiral gets confidence in you, he brings you into a lot of sensitive issues.

We had a chief of staff who was a "Captain Queeg" kind of a guy.† I kept waiting

---

* Rear Admiral Robert A. Macpherson, USN, served as Commander Anti-Submarine Warfare Group Five from August 1964 to October 1965.
† Lieutenant Commander Philip F. Queeg, USN, was the fictitious commanding officer of the destroyer-minesweeper USS Caine in Herman Wouk's classic naval novel of World War II, The Caine Mutiny, published by Doubleday & Company in 1951. Queeg was a mentally unstable martinet, so his name has become associated with overbearing, eccentric skippers.

for him to take the steel balls out of his pocket. When you sat in his office, getting the benefit of his leadership philosophy, it was just like the movie. Whenever I made a mistake, he would call me in and say, "Now, this is the way we do this." It was good that he did that, but it was the way he said it. He saw himself as one who knew Navy protocol backward and forward, and if it wasn't done precisely right, the world was going to come to an end: "You are going to have to clean up your act, or things are going to fall apart." He would sit and look at his hands to see if they were okay. His uniform was always absolutely perfect.

One of the other pains of that job was the flag mess management. Balancing the budget, collecting mess bills, trying to keep the members happy (impossible for some). You don't get many complaints from the admiral. Most of them come from the commanders and a captain occasionally. Aide duty was a learning experience and very broadening.

Paul Stillwell: What do you remember about your watchstanding on the bridge?

Admiral Osborn: Shortly after we got into the Philippine Sea area we had a major exercise with a lot of ships. We had eight destroyers in the screen. It was a pitch-black night. I gave the signal from the flag bridge for a major turn. For someone who had never been around ships, it was a stirring experience to watch that evolution, seeing ships execute precisely and others not so well. The flag bridge duty wasn't difficult unless you were in an exercise where there was a lot going on. Underway steaming with a screen was pretty routine. My watches on the ship's bridge were another story. That was very intensive. The skipper gave me some leeway. He didn't train me as hard as he did his ship's company. He did let me take the ship into Subic Bay, which was quite a thrill.

Paul Stillwell: How effective were the CVSs in the antisubmarine role?[*]

---

[*] In the 1950s a number of <u>Essex</u>-class attack carriers were converted to specialize in antisubmarine warfare and were redesignated from CVA to CVS. The last of the CVSs were phased out in the early 1970s.

Admiral Osborn: Not very effective. The S-2s had the same detection equipment as those P-2s had in my first squadron—comparative listening.* We had two CVAs and our CVS on station.† The S-2s conducted surveillance around the two CVAs, looking for patrol boats and submarines. We had a couple of A-4 jets on the CVS. They would investigate distant surface or air contacts. We had two H-3 helicopter squadrons with the early versions of dipping sonar.‡ Frankly, our H-3s were logistic platforms most of the time. When in port, the H-3s were constant flying buses. When we did an opposed sortie upon getting under way, the H-3s were too tired, maintenance wise, to be effective against any submarine.

Paul Stillwell: On the subject of your experiences in the Gulf of Tonkin and WestPac, I suspect that part of the reason that you didn't get much ASW experience is that there was virtually no threat.§

Admiral Osborn: I think that is true. On that cruise in <u>Bennington</u> the only submarine activity we had was during exercises. I don't remember of intelligence ever reporting a submarine threat. Maybe a couple of times a Soviet sub would come into that general area. We just didn't spend any time at ASW. Of course, the Tonkin Gulf water was too shallow for submarines in most places.

One thing I wanted to mention about being an aide in a carrier is the coordination involved in the job. You are kind of a liaison with the carrier CO, XO, the CAG and the navigator (who "owns" the quarterdeck) with regard to the admiral and his activities.** You learn, sometimes the hard way, to use a lot of discretion and judgment in dealing back and forth. First of all, the ship's company considers having the flag and staff aboard a pain in the neck—and it is. The navigator is responsible for the quarterdeck, but the

---

* Grumman S2F Tracker propeller-driven, carrier-based antisubmarine planes first entered fleet squadrons in early 1954. In 1962 the Tracker was redesignated S-2. The S-2E version was 44 feet long, wingspan of 72 feet, gross weight of 26,867 pounds, and top speed of 253 miles per hour.
† CVA—attack aircraft carrier.
‡ The Sikorsky SH-3 Sea King is an antisubmarine helicopter. Deliveries to the fleet began in September 1961 when it was the HSS-2; it was redesignated SH-3 in September 1962. The helo has a rotor diameter of 62 feet; length, 72 feet, 8 inches; gross weight, 18,897 pounds; top speed, 166 miles per hour.
§ WestPac—Western Pacific. The Gulf of Tonkin borders the nation of Vietnam.
** XO—executive officer; CAG—commander of the embarked carrier air wing. This abbreviation is a holdover from the period prior to 1962 when the title was carrier air group.

aide is responsible for getting the admiral through that quarterdeck and doing it right. The skipper wants to know what the admiral is thinking, so you have to decide what you tell the skipper and what you don't tell him. The CAG has to move the admiral on and off the carrier. Anything significant that the staff needs goes through the XO. It is a real push-pull position to be in, but you learn how to, and not to, coordinate and compromise with these people.

Paul Stillwell: Do you have some stories to illustrate some of these various interfaces you have described?

Admiral Osborn: The only real significant incident was during a stop at the White Beach anchorage in Okinawa. There was a small naval activity there to support ships that called at the harbor, also an officers' club and exchange. The ship's company officers migrated to the officers' club one evening. The admiral had been there earlier in the evening, departed, and I stuck around. The air wing officers got carried away and tore the place up pretty bad. I knew who had done it. I got pressed pretty hard by our chief of staff for details. I didn't tell him much of anything, but they found out from another source who the culprits were. I ended up taking the blame from the air group.

Regarding coordination with the ship, the biggest pain of all was the issue of keeping the flag space decks and passageways clean. The ship had responsibility, but they had the malcontents doing the work, so it was always a hassle. The chief of staff inspected these decks and passageways constantly. It was minutiae, and I'm not a minutiae person. It just drove me nuts. That ship was not really responsive to the flag staff in a lot of ways.

Paul Stillwell: You have given your observations of Admiral Caldwell. What about Admiral Macpherson?

Admiral Osborn: He had been the Chief of Naval Air Training and then went to Commander Patrol Forces Seventh Fleet/Taiwan Defense Force. He came from that position to be Commander ASW Group Five. He was a very quiet guy—a little too quiet and unassuming. Not quite forceful enough. A wonderful gentleman who treated me very well. I felt he could have made a greater contribution with a little more force. On the other hand, Caldwell was quiet, but he had that aura that told you he was in charge.

Paul Stillwell: Cubi Point/Subic Bay.* What can you say about that whole Subic Bay experience?

Admiral Osborn: I am showing a little of my prejudice here, but I think this Tailhook thing is related to Cubi in a way.† We have really been ill served by the tailhook community. The damage done by the Tailhook episode in Las Vegas was enormous in terms of naval aviation programs in Congress. Here you have mature, grown-up human beings who go into the Cubi O-club and act like animals. That should not have been allowed to happen. I think the Cubi O-club attitude had a tremendous influence on the tailhook fiasco. Clearly, the air group needed a way to let off steam when they came off Yankee Station, but it should have had some bounds.‡

With regard to the Tailhook convention, the tailhookers had been doing those kinds of things for years. It just hadn't received the publicity. It probably got a little worse the year it came to a head. The fact that there were female aviators involved just exacerbated the situation. We had college graduates, commissioned naval officers, who were allowed to do the kind of thing they did at the Cubi O-club. Tailhook was a shortcoming in our naval leadership. After the Tailhook incident was a matter of record,

---

* Subic Bay is a protected anchorage on the island of Luzon in the Philippines. It borders the Bataan province and is about 35 miles north of the entrance to Manila Bay. During the Vietnam War, Subic had a strong role as a support base for the U.S. Navy. Included were a naval air station, piers, ship repair facility, supply depot, and recreational outlets for ships' crews.

† Following the Tailhook Association's 1991 convention in Las Vegas, a number of women complained of being mistreated by naval officers in attendance. There were other allegations of inappropriate behavior. A long, largely inconclusive investigation followed. The upshot was damage to the Navy's overall reputation and to that of naval aviation in particular. For a detailed analysis, see "Tailhook: What Happened, Why & What's to be Learned," U.S. Naval Institute Proceedings, September 1994, pages 89-103.

‡ During the initial stages of involvement in the Vietnam War, the U.S. Navy maintained aircraft carriers on two stations based on Civil War designations—Yankee Station off North Vietnam and Dixie Station off South Vietnam. The latter, which began on 16 May 1965, was dropped 15 months later once airfields were available ashore in South Vietnam.

I heard three-star aviators talking about Tailhook in change-of-command speeches and not showing any contrition, still saying that Tailhook was no big deal.

Paul Stillwell: Do you think there was sort of an entitlement that TacAir people thought they had to break the rules?

Admiral Osborn: I think so. Like I mentioned, the leadership allowed it to happen. When the senior aviators joined in and condoned Tailhook happenings for years, it was a disaster waiting to happen.

Paul Stillwell: There was the taint on everyone who wore golden wings, whether he or she was involved or not.

Admiral Osborn: The worst part was that the naval leadership tried to sweep it under the rug. The CNO told OP-05 to do something, and he sandbagged because he had been at Tailhook and involved in parts of it.[*] If the CNO had gone to the two CinCs, and told them to run the thing to ground and take action, there might have been some scapegoats, but the overall cost would have been far less.[†] The congressional watchdogs would have backed off in the face of decisive action within the Navy.

Paul Stillwell: Anything more on Subic?

Admiral Osborn: It was a wonderful experience to go to Subic and go on liberty. You have the heartbeat of the Navy in a foreign port, Olongapo and all that stuff.[‡] Subic is a great port. There couldn't have been a better place to operate out of. A real sailors' port.

Paul Stillwell: Did you get to Japan while you were on that cruise?

---

[*] Vice Admiral Richard M. Dunleavy, USN, served as OP-05, Assistant Chief of Naval Operations (Air Warfare) from 25 May 1989 to 12 June 1992.
[†] CinCs—Commander in Chief Atlantic Fleet and Commander in Chief Pacific Fleet.
[‡] Olongapo, the town right outside the U.S. naval base at Subic Bay in the Philippines, was noted for its raunchiness during the Vietnam War period and later.

Admiral Osborn: I'll tell you a story about that—my best aide story. Admiral Macpherson, having been Commander Taiwan Defense Force during the time of Quemoy/Matsu, spent quite a bit of time in Japan and got to know the Japanese admirals of the day.* The first time we were scheduled into Yokosuka for a Seventh Fleet scheduling conference, the admiral told me to set up calls on several personages, including two admirals with headquarters near Yokosuka. After making the arrangements for the calls, I would normally have the Marine driver do a dry run to the various places for timing, etc. This time, the driver claimed he had been to the headquarters of the two admirals on a previous port visit and didn't need to do a dry run. I assumed he knew where he was going. That was the last time as an aide that I ever assumed anything.

We got in the car and proceeded to the headquarters of the admiral we were calling on. As we approached the headquarters, at the end of a long driveway, Admiral Macpherson saw that we were going to the wrong place. However, there was no place to turn around, and the sentry had already seen our sedan with the admiral's flag on the fender. He scurried into the headquarters to announce that a flag officer was approaching. We drove up to the entrance, stopped, and saw that the Japanese admiral was coming out to greet us. Fortunately he had not been occupied with another visitor. He saw who it is, was very cordial, and welcomed Admiral Macpherson. They went in and had tea, whereupon we departed. That was my worst aide mistake and almost my undoing. The admiral swallowed it but not easily.

Paul Stillwell: What happened with the other admiral? You are getting into the area of international face when you do these things.

---

* On 23 August 1958, Communist China began an intensive artillery bombardment of the offshore islands of Quemoy and Matsu, which were held by the Nationalist Chinese government. The Seventh Fleet escorted troop transports that carried forces to protect the two islands. The aircraft carrier Essex (CVA-9) supported the operation. Admiral Macpherson served as Commander Taiwan Patrol Force/Fleet Air Wing One, 1962-64.

Admiral Osborn: You know how formal the Japanese are, particularly in official matters. We went to the other admiral's office the next day. I don't know how that went, whether they shared a laugh or not, probably not.

Paul Stillwell: Do you have some positive memories from Japan during that period?

Admiral Osborn: Admiral Macpherson was wined and dined tremendously. In the evenings we had these five- or six-hour dinners with entertainment and lots of saki. That was quite a nice experience.

Paul Stillwell: I was in Japan around that time and was struck by the cordiality between the two countries whose people had been killing each other 20 or 30 years earlier.

Admiral Osborn: When, later, I was Commander Patrol Wings Pacific, we had some wonderful exchanges. Every year we had an ASW exercise at Moffett Field with the Japanese and Australians. One year the Japanese were flying six P-3s to Moffett for the exercise. There had never been a Japanese military plane land at Adak since the war ended, so I got the idea, and proposed to Third Fleet, that we bring the Japanese P-3s via Adak. This didn't seem too important to us, but to the Japanese it a big deal. So we did it. I was at Adak to greet them and then flew on a Japanese P-3 from Adak to Moffett. The Japanese Government considered it very significant. One of our squadrons was at Misawa, so I would go up there and get treated very well. That is a beautiful and much different part of Japan.

Paul Stillwell: Any other highlights from that cruise that you want to put on the record?

Admiral Osborn: As our task group was leaving Seventh Fleet en route home in October 1965, we inadvertently found ourselves on the edge of a major typhoon. The typhoon had changed direction unexpectedly, and we could not react in time to avoid the serious weather. We were in a raging storm for about two days, and the task group—carrier and eight destroyers—was getting low on fuel. At one point the carrier rendezvoused with an oiler, and they were able to make fueling connections. However, the sea was so bad that a fueling line separated and shot many gallons of black oil into the hangar deck of the carrier. It took days to clean up the mess. In the meantime, the storm was so severe that waves were breaking 50 feet above the level of the flight deck at the bow. The catwalks on both sides of the flight deck were torn off and pointed skyward. Many of the hatches and doors in the destroyers were warped so that they weren't movable. I was thrown from my bunk to the deck in the middle of the night. That kind of roll in a carrier is significant.

The last admiral I worked for was Eli Reich.[*] Have you done a history of him?

Paul Stillwell: He did an oral history with my predecessor. He was a splendid submariner and an innovator after that as well.

Admiral Osborn: He was a real light in naval history. A wonderful man. I only worked for him for about three weeks.

Paul Stillwell: What do remember of him from a three-week exposure?

Admiral Osborn: A gentlemanly person of the old school. It made you feel good to be with him. However, you could tell that he could be tough when he needed to. A well-mannered person, a lot of culture. Even though I was only a fly on the table for a three-week period, he was very good to me.

Paul Stillwell: Your next tour was with CTF 72.[†] How did that come about?

Admiral Osborn: I ended up in this job as a result of deciding for the second time in my naval career that I was going to get out of the Navy. My resignation from my regular

---

[*] Rear Admiral Eli T. Reich, USN, served as Commander Anti-Submarine Warfare Group Five from October 1965 to January 1967. The oral history of Reich, who retired as a vice admiral, is in the Naval Institute collection.
[†] Task Force 72 was the Taiwan Patrol Force, a component of the U.S. Seventh Fleet.

commission was accepted. Before I could be drummed off the ship, I changed my mind again.

Paul Stillwell: What had been the inducement to leave this time?

Admiral Osborn: Family separation had a lot to do with it. There were a lot of great experiences aboard ship, but looking down the road I saw more lengthy separations just didn't look good. I had already experienced three deployments of six months or longer plus the carrier tour. That was the big thing. My intention was to go with an airline. They were hiring like mad at that time.

Paul Stillwell: What kind of input did your wife give you on this decision?

Admiral Osborn: She thought I was making a mistake, even though she hated the separations worse than I did. During deployment the time went fast for me because of the busy schedule. Also, for the most part, I was enjoying it. She was at home with the kids, dealing with family emergencies, which always seemed to come when I was gone. When you are a wife alone, the civilian neighbors tend to shy away from you because they aren't used to that kind of thing. I think she sensed that I liked the Navy, and she was willing to accept the separations. We had a couple of long telephone conversations from the Philippines about this. In the end, I went to the admiral and told him I'd like to stay in.

In the meantime, my relief was en route, so they sent me to CTF 72, the maritime operations staff for Com7thFlt.* CTF 72 flew his flag from a seaplane tender deployed to Seventh Fleet. He would shift his flag every six months to the newly deploying tender.† We operated out of Okinawa. We eventually got quarters at Kadena Air Force Base after living on the economy for two or three months. Our household goods were misrouted by

---

* Com7thFlt—Commander Seventh Fleet.
† The three seaplane tenders that rotated in this role were the <u>Pine Island</u> (AV-12), <u>Salisbury Sound</u> (AV-13), and <u>Currituck</u> (AV-7).

the shipping company. They went from Long Beach to Singapore to Long Beach to Okinawa and took seven months to arrive.

The staff was rarely in Okinawa. Most of the time we were in or around Vietnam so that the tender could support seaplanes engaged in Market Time surveillance and interdiction operations off the coast of Vietnam.[*] The seaplanes carried .50-caliber machine guns for use against sampans carrying small arms. I'll relate an anecdote about my first flight with one of the squadrons shortly after joining the staff. The P-5 Marlin seaplanes were carrying depth bombs in addition to the machine guns, which made them quite heavy for takeoff. In order to get off the water they were using jet-assisted takeoff bottles (JATO) to augment the reciprocating engines for takeoff. I had never experienced a JATO takeoff, nor did they alert me that we were going to use it. The crew assigned me a seat in the very aft of the aircraft, next to a large observation window. When we got some speed in the takeoff run on this pitch-black night, they ignited the JATO. The explosion and flash of light next to my window was enormous and totally unexpected. I thought the plane had blown up. It was not a pleasant experience. The crew had, of course, preplanned the whole thing and got a kick out of getting the best of one of the staff officers.

My job on that staff was assistant air operations officer, which meant that I originated all the flight orders for the P-2, P-3, and P-5 operations in Seventh Fleet. Roy Isaman was the admiral.[†] He was very sharp, a bit aloof, but did a good job. His problem was that he was not well served by his chief of staff or operations officer. During my entire naval career there were three people that I didn't do well with or have any respect for. This chief of staff and the operations officer were two of them. So this was kind of a mixed experience.

This was right in the height of the Vietnam War. Our maritime aircraft were conducting heavy operations in support of the carrier divisions and Market Time off the Vietnam coast, as well as individual tasks around the whole of Seventh Fleet. CTF 77

---

[*] In the summer of 1965 U.S. ships and craft began working with the South Vietnamese Navy to establish the Market Time patrol off the coast of South Vietnam. Its purpose was to monitor coastal traffic and thus to prevent North Vietnamese craft from infiltrating South Vietnam to deliver weapons and other supplies to Viet Cong forces.
[†] Rear Admiral Roy M. Isaman, USN, served as Commander Patrol Force Seventh Fleet/Taiwan Patrol Force from 1965 to 1967.

message traffic was heavy.* You couldn't sit around and ruminate on things much. The operational pace was terrific. We would draft an air order for the next day, and the operations officer and chief of staff would spend hours with us making minor changes here and there so that the wording was to their liking. The changes were innocuous. Meanwhile, the war was continuing, and people were waiting for our messages. A policy message was doomed from the start. The chief of staff would rewrite many times over a couple of days before ever going to the admiral. He often sat three or four of us down, took out a tablet of lined paper, and rewrote the entire message over a couple-hour period. When he finished, it would say the same thing in different words. The only thing I could ever think about in those sessions was if any of the people at CTF 77 ever knew what was going on in that office, they would be absolutely right about everything they ever said about VP!

Paul Stillwell: Did the admiral know that this was going on?

Admiral Osborn: I am not sure whether he did or not. I always felt that he wasn't happy to be in that particular job—away from carrier aviation—and was leaving day-to-day operations to his chief of staff.

Paul Stillwell: One of his predecessors in that job was George Anderson, who was a very aggressive, hard-charging type.† He went on to become CNO.‡

Admiral Osborn: I am glad you mentioned George Anderson. Let me take you back for a moment to VP-31 in San Diego. I had just arrived in the squadron when word came that the CNO, Admiral George Anderson, was coming to North Island to visit. As a part of his visit to Kitty Hawk they were going to have a static display of a number of things on the hangar deck of the carrier. The Kitty Hawk was newly commissioned and based at

---

* Task Force 77 was the Attack Carrier Striking Force of the Seventh Fleet.
† Rear Admiral George W. Anderson, Jr., USN, served in the billet in 1955-56. The title was changed from Formosa Patrol Force to Taiwan Patrol Force in late 1955.
‡ As a four-star admiral, Anderson served as Chief of Naval Operations from 1 August 1961 to 1 August 1963. His oral history is in the Naval Institute collection.

North Island.* VP-31 had a "home-made" ASW trainer which had received enough attention that it was selected to be among the things to show the CNO. I was assigned to be the one to describe this trainer to him when he came around the hangar deck. I didn't know a whole lot about this gadget but had done a little homework.

All of the sudden, the entourage arrived, and here was this giant man. He seemed about eight feet tall. To this day I remember the feeling that as a lowly lieutenant if I screw this up with the CNO, my days are numbered. For some reason this thing caught his attention, and he kept asking questions which I had to manufacture answers for as quickly as possible. It seemed like he was there for an hour; it was probably more like five minutes. Afterward, they said it went okay. It sure didn't seem like it went okay to me. At that point I didn't expect to come within hearing distance of the CNO, let alone talk to him.

Paul Stillwell: How did you manage this mix of planes at CTF 72? You had land planes and seaplanes. How did you figure out who did what?

Admiral Osborn: We had P-2s at Tan Son Nhut, P-5s at Cam Ranh Bay operating off the tenders and P-3s at Cam Ranh Bay, AFB.† We had P-2s and P-3s at Sangley Point and P-3s at Naha, Okinawa.‡ We also had P-3s operating out of Iwakuni, Guam, and Misawa.

Paul Stillwell: Did you have different roles assigned to the different planes because of capability?

Admiral Osborn: Yes, except they were all doing similar missions, so it was a matter of considering time-on-station capability, which was different for the three types of aircraft. The P-5s would usually operate from Cam Ranh Bay south, the P-2s further south from Ton San Nhut, and the P-3s would take the northern sector up to and including the

---

* The aircraft carrier <u>Kitty Hawk</u> (CVA-63) was commissioned 29 April 1961.
† Tan Son Nhut was the name of the U.S. Air Force base at Saigon, South Vietnam.
‡ Sangley Point is on Manila Bay in the Philippines.

Tonkin Gulf and Yankee Station. The coordination issue was really only along Vietnam. It was not a very complicated plan to develop.

Paul Stillwell: How did the command arrangement work, because Market Time was not under Seventh Fleet?

Admiral Osborn: The Seventh Fleet staff coordinated with ComUSMACV and ComNavForV in setting the surveillance requirement.* The latter two then got on and off station reports as well as contact reports in parallel with Com7thFlt and CTF 72. Our aircraft communicated with NavForV forces as necessary while on station. We would vector ships onto suspicious contacts.

Paul Stillwell: How effective would you say that surveillance effort was?

Admiral Osborn: Any gunrunner that went out very far from the shoreline was in danger, but a lot got through without detection. My opinion is that it probably wasn't very effective over all.

Paul Stillwell: What was your support role with respect to CTF 77?

Admiral Osborn: Surface surveillance for torpedo boats around the carriers on Yankee Station. If the CVS was on station, we weren't in the area. There was not always a CVS on station because the three CVSs—Bennington, Hornet, and Kearsarge—were not providing full-time coverage.

There were two or three occasions of contact with torpedo boats. Submarines weren't considered a major threat on Yankee Station because of shallow water in most of the area. There was some concern about it, because two or three carriers together were sitting ducks. As an aside, it has always been my contention that a carrier will be torpedoed some day. It is sort of like the potential for a small, unmarked vessel of

---

* ComUSMACV—Commander U.S. Military Assistance Command Vietnam. ComNavForV—Commander U.S. Naval Forces Vietnam.

unknown origin carrying a nuclear weapon to sail up the Potomac to the basin below the District of Columbia. We have a host of countries with diesel submarines that could fire at a carrier and depart without detection. Remember, the carriers today have very limited integral ASW capability. The S-3 is slowly going away and is currently being used primarily as a tanker.* Carrier skippers don't worry a lot about submarines. They say that they do but not really. They view their carriers as invincible re submarines.

Paul Stillwell: Did you go ashore in Vietnam at all?

Admiral Osborn: Yes, but not in any risk areas. On a later tour, while flying P-3s out of Cam Ranh Bay, we had occasional ground alerts but no real threat. I was in Tan Son Nhut for staff meetings in Saigon. I was never at risk.

Paul Stillwell: What observations did you have of the local culture?

Admiral Osborn: I didn't spend enough time on the ground to get familiar with the local people. In those short visits we saw a lot of black market stands, mopeds, and motorcycles.

Paul Stillwell: Any observations about the seaplane tenders in which you lived? Certainly that is a different type of ship than an aircraft carrier.

Admiral Osborn: They were pretty well run ships. All three of the tenders had excellent skippers. They were shipshape, clean. The wardrooms were good people.

Paul Stillwell: What was the relationship between ship's company and staff?

---

* The S-3 Viking is a jet-powered, carrier-based antisubmarine aircraft with a four-person crew. Built by Lockheed, its first delivery to a fleet training squadron was in February 1974. The S-3A has a wingspan of 68 feet, 8 inches; length of 53 feet, 4 inches; maximum gross weight of 52,539 pounds, and a top speed of 514 miles per hour.

Admiral Osborn: Just like on a carrier: "When are you going to leave?" "Sure was nice before you got here." But a slightly different flavor. That was the mission of the seaplane tender, to carry the staff whenever deployed. The carriers didn't always have staff on board. The tenders knew the flag would be on board in Seventh Fleet every time.

Paul Stillwell: What kind of a command center did you have for running these operations?

Admiral Osborn: We had a flag plot room that was all paper—charts on the wall, very rudimentary, plus a secure space for back-channel traffic. There was a lot of back-channel traffic with six or eight of us cleared for the information.

Paul Stillwell: Why so much back channel?

Admiral Osborn: We were getting intell from codeword sources.

Paul Stillwell: Were there ever plans to use the patrol planes for mining?

Admiral Osborn: Yes, there were. After I was on the staff they came close to mining Haiphong with A-6s and P-3s.[*] Everyone was on alert and the mines were loaded. I believe that was about the time of B-52 extensive bombing.[†] It was going to be a high-risk operation with high attrition. That was taken as a given. I don't know what the decision process was regarding go or no go.

Paul Stillwell: My perception was that mining had the potential of causing the Chinese or Soviets to escalate the war.

---

[*] The Grumman-built A-6 Intruder was the Navy's principal carrier-based bomber from the early 1960s to the early 1990s.
[†] The Boeing B-52 Stratofortress is an eight-engine jet-propelled heavy bomber flown by the U.S. Air Force.

Admiral Osborn: That might have been, because there were a lot of ships from those countries in the harbor.

Paul Stillwell: You mentioned when we weren't recording that you had a little flight time in seaplanes. Could you say what that was?

Admiral Osborn: Back at that time if you weren't in a flying billet you had to get four hours a month of flight time in order to keep flight pay. I would go on the Market Time patrols as an observer or to spell the pilots in the crew. I was never in the cockpit for takeoff or landing.

Paul Stillwell: Do you have any other descriptions of takeoffs and landings other than the one with JATO?

Admiral Osborn: I had flown in P-5s quite a bit at VP-31. When you prepare to land, you set up a rate of descent and hold that attitude until you contact the water; then you pull the power off. Depending on sea state and the wind direction relative to the swell—if there is one—you can end up with a pretty stiff landing, or maybe two landings. The P-5 was a well-built plane that could take a pretty good beating. They couldn't make open-sea landings in the kind of conditions the PBY Catalinas could, but they were tough. Cam Ranh Bay is a fairly good size piece of water that could develop some challenging landing conditions. The P-5 was a slow, dependable ocean patrol plane. It did a good job and showed the flag in many parts of the world not accessible to land-or carrier-based planes.

Back to VP-31 for a moment, the sea-lane for the P-5 was between North Island and the city of San Diego. That stretch of water is very busy with motorboats, sailboats, U.S. Navy ships, merchant ships, etc., so landings were exciting. More than one sailboat ventured into the sea-lane at the wrong time and either got a good scare or lost its mast.

Paul Stillwell: What were the factors that phased Navy seaplanes out?

Admiral Osborn: The P-5s were getting old. They needed expensive rework in order to continue for any length of time. Seaplanes deteriorate more rapidly because of the salt water and salt air corrosion. Seaplane tenders are expensive to operate. The introduction of the P-3 was a big budget item which didn't leave any flexibility for other long-range patrol options. The 24 P-3 squadrons split evenly between the Atlantic and Pacific fleets were able to cover all the maritime requirements. The P-3 allowed surveillance of more area in the same amount of time at reduced cost. The P-3 was much longer range than either the P-2 or P-5. With the increased range, the P-3 could cover the out-of-the-way places previously reached by tender-supported P-5s.

However, even the P-3 had limitations in a few places. For example, there is an area in the Gulf of Alaska about midway between Hawaii, the Aleutians, and Seattle where a P-3 can only spend about two hours on station. The Russians knew that. They gave us fits when they were operating up there extensively. We knew from SOSUS intelligence that their SSBNs operated there, but it took a lot of P-3 assets to monitor their activity.[*] Back to seaplanes briefly, the Navy was very serious about a replacement seaplane in the '50s. Two or three P6M jet seaplanes were built and tested.[†] Testing did not go well. Salt-water corrosion plagued the engines. At least one crashed, and the program died a budgetary death.

Paul Stillwell: Was Admiral Isaman CTF 72 the whole time?

Admiral Osborn: Yes, I was only on that staff for a year. I had been selected for postgraduate education in the Naval Postgraduate School management program. They started a mid-year term in December that year for the first time and needed students for the class. On the seventh of December 1966 in Cam Ranh Bay, I received orders to be in Monterey seven days later. I flew to Okinawa; we packed out, and flew to San Francisco,

---

[*] SOSUS--sound surveillance system, a seafloor network of listening devices used by the U.S. Navy to detect noises from transiting ships. SSBN—ballistic missile nuclear-powered submarine.
[†] The Martin P6M Seamaster was a swept-wing seaplane powered by four J-71 engines. It was designed for minelaying and reconnaissance flights. It made its first flight in July 1955. Plagued by technical problems and competing priorities, the plane was limited to prototypes. It never went into production or fleet service.

then to Monterey in seven days. It was ridiculous. We had figured that we would be in Okinawa at least two years.

The year in Monterey in PG School was my only tour in the Navy which I did not enjoy. It was a good thing to do, but I was not comfortable because I had been out of college for 14 years. The highest math in my background was a college freshman algebra course. The management curriculum included differential calculus and a few other math-oriented subjects as core courses. We were required to have a cumulative B average in order to be awarded a master's degree. I studied until 11:00 or 12:00 o'clock at night Monday through Thursday. We would do something as a family on Friday night. All day Saturday was study as well as Sunday afternoon and evening. Going into the last term I had a C average and barely squeaked out a B average at the end. That was not fun.

Paul Stillwell: What else besides calculus was in the curriculum?

Admiral Osborn: Economics, macro and micro; a number of management courses, accounting, probability and statistics, a little leadership.

Paul Stillwell: Why were you in that major, per se? How did you get picked for that?

Admiral Osborn: Don't know. I had applied for PG school but hadn't indicated a preference. That was probably the only one I was qualified for due to my math background. It was probably a combination of my college background and their needing a name to put in a slot.

Paul Stillwell: Was it your incentive that this was a career-enhancing step, a ticket to be punched?

Admiral Osborn: Yes, if the Navy wanted to fund my education I wasn't going to say no. I didn't push for it.

Paul Stillwell: Did you and your family get a chance to enjoy the Monterey area?

Admiral Osborn: Not very much, actually. I was nose to the grindstone most of the time. We don't really care for Monterey; the weather tends to be cool and foggy. It is a beautiful area.

Paul Stillwell: You sort of looked at that as a thing you had to endure to get on with things that you would enjoy more.

Admiral Osborn: Yes. Of course, I didn't think about it a lot of the time. Once we got there and found out what I was up against, there was no choice but to dig in and make the most of it.

Paul Stillwell: Did the content and substance of what you learned have useful applications later in your career?

Admiral Osborn: Yes, the economics and management courses. The research experience. I ended up in the personnel business later where some of the learning applied, either directly or indirectly. It is hard to say whether the Navy got their money's worth or not.

Paul Stillwell: Did you have any subsequent specific tours of duty that constituted a payback, something you had to do that called for that specific education.

Admiral Osborn: Yes, when I left the wing commander job I went to NMPC to be the Director of Restricted Line and Staff Placement, and from there to the NMPC deputy job. After being selected for flag rank, I was the NMPC director for a few months. The PG school experience was secondarily useful in those positions.

The tour following postgraduate school was in VP-19 at Moffett Field. A prerequisite for that tour was completion of several preparatory courses at Fleet Aviation Electronics Training Pacific, located at North Island, San Diego. One of the courses was SERE school (survival, escape and evasion). All aviators are required to attend SERE school before their first squadron. The survival school I attended years earlier did not have an escape, evasion, or prisoner compound phase. That had become important and required.

At any rate, there were supposed to be three senior lieutenant commanders attending this particular school. None of those officers showed up for the course. The morning I reported they informed me that I would be the officer-in-charge of the 145 SERE students for eight days. Being the O-in-C meant just that. I was responsible for the conduct of the 145 students for the entire course. That really came into the fore during the compound phase where they simulated POW conditions.[*] They do an effective job of simulating the kind of things you are going to experience in a POW camp. They don't simulate the body stretchings and beatings experienced in Vietnam, but they do an excellent job of playing out the other aspects of torture to get you thinking about the kind of things you may be exposed to if captured. Things like extended periods in a box barely large enough for your body with your knees and toes on the floor and overhead door is pressing on your back and head. The idea is to remain there until you "break." One of the things I hated the worst was water torture. Arms and legs strapped down, flat on your back, they applied a cloth over your nose and mouth while pouring water in your face. It is sort of a feeling of combined suffocation and drowning.

The compound is a prison kind of atmosphere. This particular facility was located at Warner Springs, California, northeast of San Diego. The instructors are all well trained to play the part of prison guards. They slap you around pretty good. There is an occasional broken bone, but not often. A broken bone is accidental. They have toned it down now, but at that time we had some fellows that got banged up. The word was out beforehand that as senior officer you had better have your people totally organized in terms of who is senior, all the way up and down the line. Every single person knew who was senior to them and who was junior. They would pull someone out and put them in the "box," then take the next person down and try to get them to break the Code of

---

[*] POW—prisoner of war.

Conduct by saying that their senior had spilled his guts, so why shouldn't you?* It was all mind bending.

Well into the compound phase my number-two guy, a lieutenant commander, completely capitulated. He spilled the beans, answered every question. They were going to boot him. He would have lost his orders to the squadron as well as his flight status. Fortunately, they had a system where they talked to the senior officer—in this case, me. They asked me if I thought he was savable and should have second chance. I said yes, so they told me to get him aside and tell him the facts of life, and they would give him a second chance. That happened in four or five cases in that group. The upshot of all this was that I learned more about leadership in that week than any other specific time in my career. It was a very unique experience. I was absolutely dumbfounded when assigned as senior officer, but when it was over I felt like it was the best thing that could have happened.

Paul Stillwell: Let's go back and compare this to your experience when you were trying to quit from Aviation Officer Candidate School—the drill instructor saving you. What was your technique?

Admiral Osborn: I told the lieutenant commander that he had to get through his head that we only had a few hours left in this situation: "You are not a prisoner of the Vietnamese. You are a prisoner of these guys who are U.S. Navy people. In a few hours we are going to be on a bus to San Diego. Do you want to be on that bus as an outcast, and probably lose your flight status, or do you want to go back as a naval officer with your head held high? You can stand anything for a few more hours."

His problem was claustrophobia in the box. He said, "I can't go back in that box."

I said, "Yes you can. Go back in there and dream that you are somewhere else

---

* The Code of Conduct is a set of rules that American service personnel are expected to follow if captured. The code was established by the U.S. Department of Defense in the wake of the Korean War, in which many servicemen collaborated with the enemy and submitted to brainwashing. The code requires steadfast resistance and encourages escape if captured. In recent years the words of the code have been changed to gender-neutral language.

doing something that you like to do. When your knees start hurting, just think of something else, and before long they will be taking you out of that box." Things like that.

Paul Stillwell: You told me that a few of the members didn't make it through. What happened to them?

Admiral Osborn: I believe they were enlisted men. They were probably taken out of aviation and allowed to continue in their underlying rate. They may have been given another chance later. Possibly they were sent back to survival school for a second try. That would have been my choice for dealing with the issue. After all, this was a training evolution. No matter how you conduct that compound phase, you can never simulate what a real POW camp is like. I have asked myself many times how I would have done in a POW camp. Of course, you can't answer that question. Only the real pain and torture will bring the answer. As John McCain described in his book, he was barely alive when they started the torture.[*] His body was all broken up, and they started pulling his arms out of their sockets, etc. What is there in a person that will bring them to stick with it? Nobody knows what they have inside them until the time comes.

Paul Stillwell: You had an enormous psychological advantage in that you knew when the ending point was. They never knew.

Admiral Osborn: That is the point exactly, and that is what I have always come to in thinking about this. That SERE compound phase was a grueling experience, but, during those 20-plus hours, we knew the clock was ticking, and this would eventually end. Like McCain said, after they had been there three or four years, "Are we ever going to get out of here?" What is it that makes you stick with it? The big thing is your pride, your desire to be a man and stand up to it, to prove to them that you are better than they are. Is that

---

[*] Lieutenant Commander John S. McCain III, USN, a naval aviator, was a prisoner in North Vietnam from 1967 to 1973. He retired as a captain in 1981. He became a member of the U.S. House of Representatives in 1983 and the U.S. Senate in 1987. He described his experiences in Faith of My Fathers (New York: Random House, 1999).

enough when they are pulling your arms out of their sockets? Of course, there must be a deep-seated faith. That is the foundation.

Paul Stillwell: You draw strength from those that are in it with you. McCain said that the worst part was when he was alone.

Admiral Osborn: I've often wondered if the psychologists were able to develop a profile of failure.

Paul Stillwell: Admiral Stockdale credited some of his training in the great classics. I would expect the combination of personality on one hand, and what life experiences you have had on the other would contribute.[*] Having had that SERE training would certainly help you cope.

You went on then to VP-19, more senior than you had ever been in a squadron before. What was your job?

Admiral Osborn: Started out as administrative officer. A patrol squadron usually has about ten lieutenant commanders. There are maybe four top line jobs. The administrative officer, operations officer, maintenance officer, and training officer are probably the most important. Of those, administrative officer is at the bottom of the list. After being administrative officer for a while, I migrated to operations officer for the deployment. As administrative officer I was kind of a secretary to the CO and XO. They were both good people who taught me a lot. They confided in me and let me know what they were thinking. Bob Cooke was the XO and Frank Barker was the CO.[†]

The interesting thing here, that might be worthwhile to talk about a little, was the immediately preceding regime. Under the previous CO the squadron had won every award available. Every single junior officer who served the year with that CO got out of

---

[*] Commander James B. Stockdale, USN, eventually a vice admiral, was a prisoner of war in Vietnam from September 1965 to February 1973. He was subsequently awarded the Medal of Honor for his heroism while in prison.
[†] Commander Franklin H. Barker, USN, commanded Patrol Squadron 19 from 22 November 1967 to 22 November 1968. The executive officer, Commander Robert A. Cooke, USN, then fleeted up and commanded the squadron from 22 November 1968 to 3 December 1969.

the Navy at the first opportunity. The CO had "award fixation" and drove everyone to win those awards. Those junior officers worked hard, not because he wanted them to, but to show him they could. They despised him. If this was naval leadership, they didn't want anything to do with it.

Frank Barker, the new CO, and the XO were the right kind of people to repair the damage—except for the loss of a number of good junior officers. They showed respect for their people and brought them back together in a spirit of teamwork. It was a good, positive turnaround in terms of morale and desire to do the job for the right reasons. The previous year had been a classic example of performance for the wrong reasons. These two COs demonstrated, with different results, the enormous amount of power a CO has over his people. Even after witnessing these two COs, as well as others earlier, I didn't really appreciate what influence a CO has until I was nearly halfway through my CO tour. If you have good ideas, have your people with you, and turn them on, there is no end to the good things that can happen. Particularly, you can get them to surprise themselves and how capable they are. Along with that, you have to give them the rope to hang themselves. They aren't going to hang themselves. They are going to stretch themselves and do more than they ever thought they could do. I wish I had come to the full realization of that at an earlier point.

Paul Stillwell: There is more than one way to achieve that, obviously. The first skipper did it by driving, where you were trying to achieve it by inspiring.

Admiral Osborn: Back to VP-19. We deployed to Adak, Alaska, for what turned out to be a very successful six months. I was the operations officer. Our junior officers were a strange bunch. They were kind of mavericks. A number of them didn't fit the mold of a naval officer. They kind of wanted to do their own thing and ignore Navy customs and traditions. Two or three tried to act like hippies. They were doing some quirky things in the BOQ. The skipper told me to do something about it. That is all he said. So we had a closed-door meeting. I told them they had a right to their individualities, but they also were naval officers and were duty bound to act like naval officers. Probably none of them really changed, but from a visible standpoint they straightened up pretty well. We had a flight surgeon who was part of that group. He was a heck of a flight surgeon, but he didn't have a lot of military officer in him.

Paul Stillwell: What was the nature of the operation out of Adak?

Admiral Osborn: We were doing surveillance in the Bering Sea and along the coast of Soviet territory. We also covered the North Pacific. There was a lot of Soviet submarine activity at that time. When the Soviet submarines came out of Petropavlosk into the North Pacific the SOSUS system could track them pretty well down across the Gulf of Alaska. We would make covert contact with them several times as they went across. When they reached their East Pacific patrol area, the Moffett P-3s would keep track of them. From that general period on to the end of the cold war we aggressively tracked the Soviet attack and ballistic missile submarines. They operated their Victor-class attack submarines off the Puget Sound in order to intercept our ballistic missile boats as they departed on patrol.* The Puget Sound entrance area was a very difficult place to prosecute their Victors because they were so quiet and SOSUS didn't cover that area. By this time, the P-3 equipment plus training and know-how had made us pretty good at our job

Paul Stillwell: Could you assign a percentage success rate?

Admiral Osborn: Initial contact depended on the accuracy of the intelligence. SOSUS was a very good cueing system. Once we gained contact on an SSBN in the patrol area, we could pretty well stay with him. The Victors were a different story—very quiet, and a very difficult target. Percentage of success against the SSBNs was pretty good. With regard to the Victor, ability to make initial contact was one thing. Ability to track for any length of time was much different. Attaining initial contact was in the neighborhood of

---

* Soviet Victor I-class nuclear-powered attack submarines entered active service at a rate of two a year from 1968 to 1975. They displaced 4,300 tons on the surface and 5,100 tons submerged; length, 312 feet; beam, 33 feet; draft, 23 feet; speed 30 knots. They were armed with torpedoes and SS-N-15 surface-to-surface missiles.

25%. Once we held solid contact, we could usually hold on for a credible period of time, certainly enough time launch an attack in a hot war situation.

Paul Stillwell: Could you work in conjunction with surface ships?

Admiral Osborn: We could when they were there, which wasn't very often. Later, when I was Commander Patrol Wings Pacific we experienced the ultimate in that regard. Com3rdFlt had formed a surface action group of about 12 frigates and destroyers under the command of Rear Admiral Jonathan Howe.* The frigates were equipped with towed arrays and most of the ships had ASW helicopters on board. The Soviets were conducting a major exercise in the Eastern Pacific. Our P-3s held contact with six Soviet submarines concurrently at one point. The mix, if I remember right, was one Echo, three Deltas, and two Victors.† We were able to turn over contact on some of these to the surface units. Contact with that many submarines in one theater of the Pacific was probably a post-World War II record. Not too long after that, the Berlin Wall came down, and the Cold War thaw began.‡

Going back to VP-19, we were doing a lot of prosecutions of SSBNs when they were in their Eastern Pacific patrol boxes. They had two boxes, or areas, for patrol, a northern and a southern box. SOSUS would track them across the northern Pacific until they entered one of these boxes, whereupon we would begin prosecution and then track them nearly full time. There were variations of when and how we would begin prosecution so as not to compromise SOSUS capability.

---

* Com3rdFlt—Commander Third Fleet. Rear Admiral Jonathan T. Howe, USN, Commander Cruiser-Destroyer Group Three from 1984 to 1986.
† Soviet Echo II-class nuclear-powered, guided missile submarines entered active service from 1962 to 1967. They displaced 5,000 tons on the surface and 6,000 tons submerged; length, 377 feet; beam, 30 feet; draft, 25 feet; speed 23 knots. They were armed with torpedoes and surface-to-surface missiles. Delta I-class nuclear-powered ballistic missile submarines entered active service from 1972 to 1977. They displaced 9,000 tons on the surface and 11,750 tons submerged; length, 459 feet; beam, 39 feet; draft, 28 feet; speed 25 knots. They were armed with torpedoes and ballistic missiles.
‡ In 1961 the East German regime built a wall that separated the Soviet- and NATO-controlled sectors of the city of Berlin. It was a symbolic gesture at the height of the Cold War. A number of East Germans were killed in subsequent escape attempts. On the night of 9 November 1989 the East German government suddenly and unexpectedly opened the wall to permit free transit. The wall was subsequently torn down, this time a symbol of the easing of relations between the superpowers.

Paul Stillwell: When I was in Officer Candidate School one of the worst threats those in charge could make was that we would be sent to Adak, Alaska. You were deployed there. What was it like?

Admiral Osborn: I deployed to Adak for all or part of four different approximately six-month deployments. Also later, Adak came under my command as ComPatWingsPac. So I saw it as a user and as an "owner" and thus got to know the place pretty well. At the time of my first deployment in 1958, the facilities were very austere and crude. There was no SOSUS station at that time. In fact, during that deployment we dropped practice depth charges at precise points to calibrate and assist in determining the optimum later location of the SOSUS arrays. We didn't know why we were dropping them at the time. We dropped where told and could only wonder what the purpose was.

Back to Adak. Reeve Aleutian Airways had the contract for air supply of the island. Reeve is a story in itself. Mr. Reeve was a bush pilot in Alaska in the early flying days and made an enormous contribution to the World War II war effort. He eventually formed the airline that flew over all of Alaska. Adak is a very difficult field to fly into and out of. In those days the electronic navigation aids and weather forecasting were pretty rudimentary. Adak is one of the most difficult fields in the world. Storm systems that originate in Siberia are very hard to predict, even with today's meteorological equipment, because they behave erratically as they come into the Bering Sea and proceed up the Aleutian chain.

Stepping back, during World War II the Army Air Corps flew P-38 fighters out of Adak. The P-38 was a high-performance, unstable plane. The only navigation aid was a beacon. They would fly missions to the west Aleutian Islands, shoot up the Japanese, and return. Their chances of visually sighting Adak upon return were almost nil. They performed various kinds of descents in the clouds, using the beacon to try to locate the runway. There were P-38 crash sites all around the area. Other planes had the same problem. A book called The Thousand Mile War is an excellent account of World War II action in the Aleutians.

Now there are modern landing systems, but Adak is still a difficult place to operate. The physical plant—buildings and facilities—are operated and maintained by civil service employees. Many lived there for years and became fixtures. They were good people but tended to be a bit reactionary toward any CO who wanted to make significant changes. Adak does not get a lot of visibility in the Pentagon or Congress, so the base is not well funded. Also, things deteriorate rapidly due to the weather conditions and salt air. Construction and maintenance costs are high because of the remoteness to continental U.S. The only trees are a few that were planted around 40 years ago to establish the "Adak National Forest." They are only four or five feet high due to the harsh environment.

The environment is very unforgiving. It is not advisable to go out alone into the tundra, because the weather can change dramatically in a few minutes. Hikers are advised to notify the authorities before departure with their planned route of travel. It is a beautiful place in its own way. Spectacular scenery. Thousands of bald eagles reside in the Aleutian chain. Hunting and fishing were the favorite pastimes of the residents. During the Cold War a very important Naval Security Group Activity unit operated on the island.[*] That, along with the SOSUS station, and the ability to operate maritime patrol aircraft, made Adak a key Cold War base. The location was strategically very important as the only location with significant infrastructure in the Aleutians. Shemya, to the west, can host aircraft operations but has limitations with respect to facilities and operating conditions.

Paul Stillwell: What were the living conditions like when you were not operating?

Admiral Osborn: We had an acceptable BOQ and fairly decent barracks, but not good. Living was difficult for the enlisted men if they didn't like the outdoors. We allowed beer in the barracks, and it worked reasonably well. The O-club was co-located with the BOQ. Families stationed there had medium-quality quarters. They didn't look very good on the outside, because there were no lawns or yards, just rocks and gravel. The school system, a part of the state school system, was excellent. The Alaska schools enjoy good

---

[*] Adak is on Andreanof Island.

funding due to state oil revenues. When I first went there, a number of World War II Quonset huts were still standing.* You could find all kinds of leftover issue gear in the huts.

Paul Stillwell: Did the wind condition known as williwaws make flying difficult?

Admiral Osborn: You don't find williwaws at Adak as often as places like Kodiak. The first time I deployed to Alaska we were based at Kodiak and flew our missions out of Adak. The williwaws at Kodiak could be ferocious. Winds could go from 30 knots to 100 or 110 knots in a few minutes. Airplanes always required extra tiedowns when parked on the ramp. Frequently the high winds prevented landing. There is only one runway at Kodiak. Landings were one direction and takeoffs the opposite direction, so wind was a major factor in flight operations. The landing runway has a mountain at the far end. This prevents wave-off as you near touchdown. Shortly after I detached from VP-17, one of the crews tried to wave off too late and crashed into the mountain.

Paul Stillwell: What about fog as a problem for operations?

Admiral Osborn: Fog is a problem at Kodiak but even more of a problem at Adak. You can have fog and 50-knot wind at the same time at Adak. Fog combined with a high cross wind can be very exciting, especially if your fuel reserve is very close to the amount necessary to reach an alternate. Also, high wind at Adak means extreme turbulence because of the hills and mountains which surround the field. You must depend on your instruments, but they can be bouncing around so much that you can hardly follow them. Those conditions accelerate your learning process.

Paul Stillwell: What was your specific role as operations officer? You scheduled the flights. What else?

---

* A Quonset hut is a semi-cylindrical metal building that can be shipped to an advance base area and erected quickly.

Admiral Osborn: We did the operational planning. In the case of submarine prosecution, we laid out the flight sequence, the crews to participate, intelligence development, and flight debriefing.

Paul Stillwell: How was the maintenance support? You said that was one of the important jobs in the squadron.

Admiral Osborn: Adak got some priority for P-3 parts because it was a strategic mission. We did pretty well support-wise. I can't speak for periods after that. There have been budget cuts which have had serious impact on parts support for all planes, not just the P-3.

Paul Stillwell: Anything else to mention on that squadron?

Admiral Osborn: Yes, one more thing. I learned a lesson as operations officer in that squadron. Up until that time, when I wanted a job done right, I did it myself. There weren't enough hours in the day, but I was trying. All these people working for me were getting very disgruntled because they weren't given any responsibility. It didn't take too long to figure out that I better start delegating or I was going to kill myself, along with having a lot of unhappy people. It also quickly became apparent that the more you delegate, the better your officers do and the more capable they become.

Paul Stillwell: Any examples of the kind of things you learned to delegate?

Admiral Osborn: Message origination, scheduling, a wide range of time-consuming things. One of the hardest things for anybody to learn is to write well. Most people think they are good writers but really are not. You have to let these people stumble through and learn from their mistakes. Otherwise, they are going to be poor writers forever. In a later job, a senior lieutenant commander named Jim Sinz brought me a memo which was poor work for a fourth grader.* Nobody had ever taken him to task and required that he

---

* Lieutenant Commander James P. Sinz, USN.

learn how to write. His personality made people think that he would never be able to write. Not so. He learned how to write. By the way, he is one of my all-time favorite officers because of his leadership talent and other positive attributes.

Paul Stillwell: On this business of delegating, I think I heard something that Eisenhower once said, "You come to the point where you learn how to sign things that you could have done better yourself but you don't have time to do."[*]

Admiral Osborn: You ask yourself, "Is changing that really going to have a significant effect on its purpose, or if I leave it this way is it going to embarrass us when the reader reads it?"

Paul Stillwell: How did you go about getting back out to the Midwest to Kansas near your roots of boyhood?

Admiral Osborn: While in VP-19, I was selected for promotion to commander and also for command of a patrol squadron. The patrol squadron command slot was a year away. The detailer had to fill a Navy slot at the Army Command and General Staff College (CGSC) at Fort Leavenworth, Kansas. I was one of four naval officers in the class of '70-71. CGSC is mid-career formal education for Army officers, normally majors. That year there was a higher number of lieutenant colonels than majors because the Vietnam War had delayed their coming. We also had 189 foreign officers in the class. These foreign officers were very carefully handpicked by their governments. Frequently the foreign officer graduates go on to be the senior military officer of the country or a high government official. It was a wonderful experience to meet and talk with these foreign students.

Paul Stillwell: Do you remember any specific instances in that regard?

---

[*] Dwight D. Eisenhower served as President of the United States from 20 January 1953 to 20 January 1961.

Admiral Osborn: There were two or three Jordanian officers in the course. An Israeli officer was in my section whom I got to know quite well. If he and I met a Jordanian in the hallway there was absolutely no recognition exchanged—as if no one was there. The Israeli went on to be one of the most decorated officers of the Israeli Army of that era.

Each CGSC section consisted of around 25 officers. Included were two or three foreign officers and two or three U.S. "other service" officers. We conducted a number of classroom maneuvering problems, including movement of field armies across the face of Europe. There were a number of courses, including leadership, psychological warfare, deception, public relations, etc. We studied a number of actual battles, including mistakes made and lessons learned. One of my responsibilities was to educate the class about the U.S. Navy. Over the course of a year I learned that Army officers are good administrators. They also have more leadership experience, because they start to gain command time at the company level. As a group they made a good impression. They worried too much about rank and precedence. They are somewhat stilted in that regard, even more so than the Navy.

Paul Stillwell: Were you treated as an outsider?

Admiral Osborn: No, I was treated very well. They seemed to enjoy having "other service" classmates. The Army officers took the course very seriously. They all had to work hard for grades because their grades and class standing went into their efficiency reports. I didn't study as hard as they did but certainly attempted to hold my own.

The Calley trial took place during that year, so there was a lot of hallway discussion of that issue.[*] Some made the case for "action in the heat of battle." The majority condemned his actions. There were a lot of battle-tested veterans in the class, officers who had been a part of tragedies and seen a lot of men die. Most didn't want to talk about their experiences. I would not have been surprised if they had looked down on me because of lack of battle experience. They did not and could not have been more

---

[*] On 29 March 1971 a court-martial convicted Army First Lieutenant William L. Calley, Jr., of premeditated murder of 22 South Vietnamese as the result of his unit's massacre of civilians in the village of Mylai on 16 March 1968. On 31 March Calley was sentenced to life imprisonment; on 20 August his sentence was reduced to 20 years.

cordial. They were very interested in the Navy and what they could learn from our association. It was a nice experience. The top student that year was a Marine, the first time that had happened. I was frankly surprised that they let it happen.

Paul Stillwell: What was the format for the teaching? A lot of lectures?

Admiral Osborn: A lot of lectures and classroom field problems. All the instructors were Army.

Paul Stillwell: Did you have guest speakers?

Admiral Osborn: Yes. They were all very good.

Paul Stillwell: Comparing this with your school experience at Monterey, which did you feel was more useful?

Admiral Osborn: Monterey was more useful, but I certainly learned a lot at CGSC. Most of the material had no direct benefit to me as a naval officer. The interplay with the other students and the leadership aspects were valuable. Later, in Washington, it was amazing how many times I did business with some of the students. If either party needed something, they usually got it. Also, as you say, another benefit is experiencing a different way of dealing with problems, of thinking differently. The Army is much more structured.

Paul Stillwell: I have heard it expressed that in the Army you can do things if they are spelled out, and in the Navy you can do things unless they are prohibited.

Admiral Osborn: Interesting that you bring that out. Recently I saw Colin Powell's list of ten life guidelines on the Internet.[*] One of them goes something along the line of, "If

---

[*] General Colin L. Powell, USA, served as Chairman of the Joint Chiefs of Staff from 1 October 1989 to 30 September 1993. In 2001 he became the first black person to serve as Secretary of State.

there is something you want to do and you are not sure if it would be approved, don't ask; just take a risk and do it." That has been one of my "isms" for years. I sent that Powell list to our children, and one of my sons came back with his favorite, which was the one I just mentioned. As you put it, Paul, it is better to ask forgiveness than permission.

Paul Stillwell: You next got command. Did it live up to the expectations you had built in the time leading up to that?

Admiral Osborn: Yes, definitely. My three command tours were the easiest jobs I ever had. I tried to let the people below me do the work with a little bit of steering and decision-making. That made it easy. Put another way, I felt the most comfortable during those three tours. In that regard, I saw COs and higher-level commanders who were not comfortable. They couldn't wait for it to be over. Command was a great experience. This command, VP-40, was an interesting story because of recent squadron history.

The CO who was leaving at the time I became executive officer was Jack Weir.[*] He had taken the job of executive officer on short notice a little over a year before when the current XO was summarily relieved. He had flown a P-3 into trees at the top of a hill in the traffic pattern at Utapao, Thailand. At that time VP-40 was widely considered as the worst VP squadron in the Pacific. Weir took over as XO for two months, followed by command for a year. In that time he turned the squadron from being the worst to being one of the best. That is an example of what the right leader can do. He later had command of Naval Air Station Keflavik, Iceland, and did a similar thing there. He was a dynamo. He wasn't very popular because he worked people hard, but no harder than he worked. He was very effective and enjoyed the respect of the officers and men.

His XO was Commander Ron Narmi.[†] I was Narmi's XO and then took command. It was a good two years. The squadron won a lot of awards—in fact, most of the awards available—and had a great reputation. We were based at Moffett Field, California. The mission was similar to what it had been in my previous tour in VP-19.

---

[*] Commander Jack Tex Weir, USN, served as commanding officer of Patrol Squadron 40 from March 1971 to February 1972.
[†] Commander Ronald E. Narmi, USN, commanded Patrol Squadron 40 from February 1972 to February 1973.

We prosecuted Soviet Yankee and Delta SSBNs when at Moffett.* We deployed to Iwakuni, Japan, where about 60% of our flying was out of Cam Ranh Bay, Vietnam. The remainder was in the Sea of Japan conducting ocean surveillance.

Paul Stillwell: What would you say about your subordinates who supported you during this time?

Admiral Osborn: They were an average group of guys with some exceptional people mixed in. The tactical coordinator of my flight crew, Tom Carper, served two terms as governor of Delaware and is now a U.S. Senator.† He was exceptional. Not one of my favorite politicians, but an exceptional person. He was very intelligent, an exceptional tactical coordinator. He trained the tactical crew well and was very adept at using the full capability of the airplane to find the submarine.

It might be worthwhile to describe the evolution of the flight crew from the old P-2 days to the then current P-3. In the P-2 days the officer crew was made up of pilots. Pilots flew the plane and also did the navigation. There were a very few naval aviation observers (NAOs) who were not qualified pilots but performed as navigators. That NAO designation evolved into the naval flight officer (NFO) designation. NFOs are officers specifically trained to do the tactical coordination of the mission in the back of the plane. The P-2 did not have a tactical coordinator function. The P-3 has a tactical coordinator (TACCO) and an assistant tactical coordinator. These two officers are not rated pilots. Their role is to lead the tactical crew in performance of the plane's mission. The assistant tactical coordinator is the navigator and communicator.

The TACCO runs the tactical problem. The enlisted crew is under his direction. He tells the pilots where to fly and manages the entire tactical situation. Tactical coordinators are exposed to a specific training curriculum to prepare them for the job, and they are very professional. The command structure in VP is such that about half of the

---

* Soviet Yankee I and Yankee II-class nuclear-powered submarines entered active service from 1967 to 1974. They displaced 7,900 tons on the surface and 9,600 tons submerged; length, 426 feet; beam, 39 feet; draft, 28 feet; speed 27 knots. They were armed with torpedoes and ballistic missiles.
† Lieutenant Thomas R. Carper, USN. He later served as Governor of Delaware from 19 January 1993 to 3 January 2001. He entered the U.S. Senate in 2001.

commanding officers at any one time are NFOs. Usually either the CO or XO is a pilot and the other is an NFO. That way, one of the two top officers is the "senior pilot" of the squadron.

Paul Stillwell: How much had the equipment and capability changed from the P-2 days?

Admiral Osborn: A lot. The P-3 has a computer—a processor—that processes the data from a number of sophisticated sensors to localize the submarine.

Paul Stillwell: What makes some people better at sniffing out submarines?

Admiral Osborn: I don't know the answer to that. It is probably part intelligence and part common sense. I've seen a lot of intelligent guys who had no common sense. It is the ability to take a lot of inputs, mesh that together with previous experience, and make the right decisions on what to do next. You also have to be decisive and act quickly when prosecuting a submarine because they move fast and evade well. People skills are important—the ability to motivate the sensor operators and get their best performance. I have seen TACCOs that the crew members hated, and therefore they didn't communicate and offer the information that was in front of them. That happens in ships too and maybe submarines. I don't know a lot about submarines, but I do know submariners. I have always felt the submarine community was by far the most professional arm of the Navy.

Paul Stillwell: With the right leadership skills, the subordinates want to make that person look good.

Admiral Osborn: Yes, because that guy will make them look good when he gets the opportunity. Everybody needs a little stroking. Anybody who says they don't like to be stroked is lying.

Nine days after I took command of VP-40, my maintenance officer, a lieutenant commander, took a plane out on a test flight. Against regulations he had a second mechanic in the flight engineer seat for takeoff. On the takeoff roll, an engine malfunctioned with all indications showing on the instruments. Instead of aborting the takeoff on the runway, they took off and eventually shut down the engine. When they got back on the ground there were indications of fire in the engine. They were lucky a turbine did not blow up, which could have led to a catastrophic fire. One of my standardization officers happened to be on board to give a qualification check to a crew member and observed what had happened during takeoff.

After landing I asked the plane commander to come to my office and tell me what happened. I asked him if there were any indications of malfunction during the takeoff, and he replied no. I had a sense that something was not right. Shortly after, the standardization officer told me that the second mechanic was in the seat for takeoff and that there was a lot of confusion during the takeoff roll. I then called the plane commander and the flight engineer into my office and asked them who was in the flight engineer seat for takeoff. The flight engineer replied that he was. I then asked the plane commander who was in the flight engineer seat for takeoff and he answered the same way. I then asked when the engine problem developed. They both replied, "After we got airborne."

At that point I informed them that they were relieved of their flight duties for lying to me and to stand by for further action. Later, I convened a field naval aviator evaluation board, which is the process for determining the fitness of a pilot to continue to fly. I also took his plane commander designation and had him transferred out of the squadron. This created quite a stir with the wing commander and the admiral, as well as some second-guessing. They probably thought I was a little too severe. The aftermath was interesting, because it sent a signal to the squadron that I didn't mess around when it came to safety. We didn't have any more dumb things happen in the airplane. It got everybody's attention and turned out to be a very positive thing. It wasn't a positive thing for those two people, but they had made their own bed.

Paul Stillwell: What kind of setup did you have to involve the families in the life of the squadron, both at Moffett and on deployment?

Admiral Osborn: We had an active program in that regard. We had an ombudsman who was the wife of a senior enlisted man. She had a direct line to the CO if she had an issue to resolve. The wives had a call tree for passing information. There was an enlisted wives' club and an officer wives' club. We also conducted briefings for the families prior to deployment. The briefings were intended to expose the families to a number of potential issues that might surface so they would be better prepared for the deployment period. They were offered advice about putting financial affairs in order, how to contact their spouse, what kind of family incidents could be expected to bring the husband home, etc. They were advised to contact the ombudsman if they were not satisfied with the response they received in emergency situations. We paid a lot of attention to family issues, particularly enlisted matters.

Paul Stillwell: What kind of issues did the ombudsman bring to you?

Admiral Osborn: One example was a case where a husband was sent home on emergency leave to deal with a family crisis. If he decided he needed to stay home past his authorized leave, the ombudsman would act as a liaison to sort out the correct action. The CO would rely on her assessment of the situation. Another example would be a crisis at home that the husband knew about, but was more or less ignoring. The ombudsman would contact the CO for assistance. The ombudsman was an important link when the normal system wasn't working for one reason or another.

Paul Stillwell: One of the responsibilities of the commanding officer is discipline. You have described the case with your maintenance officer. What about dealing with the enlisted members of the squadron?

Admiral Osborn: Nobody wanted to come to mast.* They didn't want to go to XO screening either, because both of us were pretty tough. The XO had a lot of leeway to

---

* Captain's mast is a sort of court in which the commanding officer of a unit listens to requests, awards non-judicial punishment, or issues commendations. Most often captain's mast is used for punishment of lesser offenses than those that merit courts-martial

take care of things. He and I had worked out our mast roles pretty carefully, and I trusted his judgment completely. If something came to XO screening, it had some substance. The weight of evidence was there. I never held mast on the hangar deck. I saw a lot of that and was not comfortable with it. Instead, I held mast in my office with an open door so anyone could come if there was room. I didn't have a lot of masts. We really didn't have a lot of XO screenings either, although they outnumbered captain's masts.

We had a couple of drug issues where the sailors involved were hammered pretty hard. Drug screening was just beginning to be well formalized. We were just starting random screening. There were administrative problems with the drug samples. The Navy hospital mixed up some samples, which nullified some convictions, but the system eventually solidified.

Paul Stillwell: That was before the zero tolerance policy came out.

Admiral Osborn: That was also the period when the CNO, Admiral Zumwalt issued his initial Z-grams, including his hair policy.[*]

Paul Stillwell: What impact did they have on the squadron?

Admiral Osborn: The sailors loved them. The way his Z-grams were worded, he was telling the sailors that he wanted them to feel good about the Navy, and he wanted them to be treated as people. He wanted to get rid of the "chickenshit regs." They loved that statement. They really liked the death of the liberty card. That one had an important message. It really said that we were placing more trust in the men. They liked the hair regulations. I, and many other COs had a problem with the hair regulations because the guidelines were not clear. The non-conformists took advantage and always erred the wrong way. It made personal appearance a hard issue to deal with.

---

[*] Z-grams were consecutively numbered policy directives from Chief of Naval Operations Zumwalt that attempted to deal with such issues as enlisted rights and privileges, equal opportunity, and Navy families. Junior personnel viewed them much more favorably than did their seniors. See U.S. Naval Institute Proceedings, May 1971, pages 291-298.

Paul Stillwell: How about greater opportunities for blacks and women? Did that have much effect right away?

Admiral Osborn: No, when I was CO we had a number of black enlisted but only one black officer. He was a problem. I expect the record would show that he met a number of hurdles in his military education and training because he was black. That was the way he looked at things: "I'm black, so I should be given the benefit of the doubt." He had trouble qualifying as a pilot and was a challenge in a number of ways.

Paul Stillwell: There were very few women in naval aviation at that time.

Admiral Osborn: Yes, the first time in my experience was later as the wing commander at Brunswick Naval Air Station. We had one of the two East Coast test squadrons for women. There were 50 carefully screened women in each squadron. They did very well.

Paul Stillwell: Any parts to wrap up on the squadron command experience?

Admiral Osborn: We had a lot of esprit de corps in the squadron. I bought an old pickup, with a cap on the back, to drive to work. During a ten-day trip overseas, some of the squadron members stole my pickup and completely redecorated it with squadron colors and insignia. They presented it to me at quarters the first morning back. That was a big deal for them. I had to drive that awful looking thing around Silicon Valley for a year. I didn't dare take anything off. That thing became very famous.

Interview Number 2 with Rear Admiral Oakley E. Osborn, U.S Navy (Retired)

Date: Friday, 6 October 2000

Place: United States Naval Institute

Interviewer: Paul Stillwell

Paul Stillwell: Let's proceed to your duty in the Pentagon and OP-594.

Admiral Osborn: Stepping back a minute, my command tour in VP-40 was cut short by two months to take this job—much against my wishes, because I was about to take the squadron on deployment. The detailer said he had to fill this job immediately, and there wasn't much choice.

I came to the job having never had any experience in Washington. I reported in, only to find that my seniors would not have cared if I reported two or three months later. I guess that illustrates the ways of BuPers sometimes.[*]

Paul Stillwell: Which just increased your sense of frustration.

Admiral Osborn: It did because it just happened that this was in the midst of the '73 gas war.[†] On top of everything else in this strange new environment, we had to sit in gas lines for hours on our allotted days. Our home was in Alexandria, quite a drive from the Pentagon, and I was absolutely lost, as everybody is the first time they report to the Pentagon. Fortunately, my fellow officers in the office were very helpful and made me feel somewhat comfortable.

My responsibilities were training and readiness, that is, I was responsible for VP and VS fleet readiness training.[‡] More particularly, I sort of became the simulator czar for the office, although there were others working in that area. At this point, we were

---
[*] BuPers—Bureau of Naval Personnel.
[†] In the winter of 1973-74 OPEC, the Organization of Petroleum Exporting Countries, initiated an embargo on delivery of Middle East oil to the West. The result was a dramatic jump in oil prices and long lines of cars at U.S. gasoline pumps in early 1974.
[‡] VS—carrier-based antisubmarine warfare aircraft.

introducing a new generation of simulators which took advantage of digital technology from both the tactical and pilot standpoint. The first digital imagery of the runway environment was available which allowed a degree of pilot training in the landing area.

A very interesting tradeoff had just taken place in the procurement of the new S-3 Viking carrier-based antisubmarine airplane. During the procurement process, the Navy sacrificed procurement dollars for four airplanes in order to purchase that value of simulators. This meant that the simulators would be fully funded and in operation concurrent with aircraft delivery—a significant step in accelerating training and readiness in the early part of fleet introduction. Otherwise, it would have been a piecemeal program, scratching like always to purchase training capability. Training normally takes last position in priority for dollars.

Paul Stillwell: I remember sitting in an S-3 simulator in 1976 and being overwhelmed by the sense of authenticity, even to the point that you heard the wheels when they went over cracks in the runway pavement.

Admiral Osborn: Singer Corporation (formerly Singer-Link) at that time had nearly a lock on simulator manufacture for the military, particularly in aviation. Their history went back to the first usable pilot trainer, the Link trainer, developed by Mr. Link, and affectionately known as the "idiot box."[*] It was a small, two-dimension box that simulated instrument conditions. An excellent trainer for its time, but not loved by pilots because it was very humbling. Anyway, Singer had developed a very strong position in the industry and, frankly, had become fairly heavy-handed in their dealings with the government. They were suffering from lack of competition in terms of quality, price, and follow-on support.

We had a lot of problems with those simulators. I remember going to McDonnell Douglas and looking at a visual system they had developed.[†] It was really the first

---

[*] Edwin A. Link, Jr. (1904-1981) was a pioneer in the field of designing flight simulators. He built his first pilot trainer in 1929 to cut down on training costs and improve flight instruction. He served as chairman of the board and president of Link Aviation, Inc., of Binghamton, New York. He later developed diving systems and submersibles.
[†] McDonnell Douglas of St. Louis was for many years a manufacturer of Navy aircraft. In August 1997 it was absorbed into the Boeing Corporation.

capable system with a computer-generated image of the runway environment. They had developed an aircraft carrier scene which was quite good for that time and far superior to Singer's offering. Evans and Sutherland, a start-up company in Salt Lake City, had just introduced a competitive system. They are now among the leaders in military simulation.

It was quite interesting to work through that time frame in terms of simulation. We did the first calculations to substitute simulator hours for flight hours in the fleet readiness squadrons. This was the first of many shock waves for pilots as flight hours have been incrementally reduced in favor of simulation. Aviators at that time said you could never substitute simulator hours for flight hours. Pilots love to fly airplanes. They don't feel quite the same about simulators! This substitution has reached the point today, with budget reductions, of leaving very few hours in the airplane for training. It is convenient for the budgeteers to say we can do it in the simulator.

Paul Stillwell: Do you have a good feel for what would be a good balance between simulator time and actual flight time?

Admiral Osborn: At that time our goal was 25% simulator time. I don't know what it is now, but I suspect it is somewhat higher than that. Today, the airlines are doing over 90% of their training in the simulator. The Navy could do that for control of the aircraft on takeoff and landing, except the carrier environment. The tactical situation is where a good deal of the training must be in actual flight. I can't see where you should go more than 35 or 40% and really be effective.

Paul Stillwell: How did you get the helicopters mixed in with that?

Admiral Osborn: They were farther back in the process. At the time they were just beginning to make real progress in helicopter simulators. They didn't have a good simulator until quite some time later.

Paul Stillwell: How did that get in your purview? You didn't have a helicopter background.

Admiral Osborn: We had three officers in OP-594: the training and readiness branch, working simulator requirements; a helicopter pilot, Dick Bruning; a TacAir pilot, Neil Campbell; and myself.[*] We all worked together. I spent a good share of my time on all the simulation issues.

Paul Stillwell: Was bringing the S-3 into the fleet a major part of your effort?

Admiral Osborn: Only from the standpoint that I dealt with the simulator issue for the VS readiness squadrons (RAG), particularly the one in San Diego.[†] They started out with a single-site RAG. Eventually there was a modified RAG at Cecil Field.[‡] I was not the primary person in the process but did spend a significant amount of time on S-3 simulation.

Paul Stillwell: Could you talk a little about the process by which a simulator gets developed. Where do all the inputs come from that go into the piece of equipment?

Admiral Osborn: It is very evolutionary, particularly in the case of fixed-wing aircraft. The Naval Training Equipment Center (NTEC) in Orlando is the command responsible for developing the technical specs of simulators. OpNav receives the requirements from the fleet (the users) and coordinates with the Naval Air Systems Command (NavAir).[§] The requirement is then passed to NTEC for development. Usually we are talking about improvements to current capabilities, except for a new airframe procurement. NTEC then issues a request for proposals (RFP) to industry. The responses are evaluated by NTEC in coordination with NavAir. Budget constraints are always a factor in deciding what to go ahead with.

---

[*] Commander Richard A. Bruning, USN; Commander Neil V. Campbell, USN.
[†] RAG—replacement air group was a term formerly used for a squadron that trains pilots and other flight crew members in a specific type of aircraft before the personnel report to a fleet squadron that flies the particular plane. The former RAGs are now known as fleet replacement squadrons.
[‡] Cecil Field is part of Naval Air Station Jacksonville, Florida.
[§] OpNav—the extended staff of the Chief of Naval Operations.

Paul Stillwell: Presumably with a new aircraft, the simulator manufacturer would work hand in hand with the aircraft manufacturer.

Admiral Osborn: Yes, they work very closely, and it is not always an easy process to fold everything together. Many times, data supplied by the aircraft manufacturer proved to be inaccurate, so the simulator didn't respond (feel) like the aircraft. Those kinds of corrections add to the frustration and cost. I don't know of a case where the aircraft manufacturer has also been the simulator supplier.

Paul Stillwell: Then you have to have some test pilots to fly the simulator, presumably.

Admiral Osborn: Yes, the Naval Air Test Center pilots and fleet pilots get involved. Over the years, teams representing all interests have come to be a relatively efficient way to shepherd simulators through development, testing, and fleet introduction.

Paul Stillwell: What do you recall about fleet replacement squadrons.

Admiral Osborn: The fleet replacement squadrons, about this time, were really beginning to show their value in terms of training and readiness—also standardization and safety. Standardization was a big issue. Stepping back, during my tour in VP-31, the VP readiness squadron, the Naval Air Training and Operations Procedures System (NATOPS) was introduced. That was also about the time it was introduced for TacAir operations. The change in accident rate was remarkable. The angled deck was the first thing in naval aviation that made a pronounced difference in accident rate.[*] The next big thing that made a difference was the NATOPS program. The readiness squadrons were responsible for managing those procedures and ensuring the fleet squadrons were following them. That has been a very successful process. Also, the implementation of fleet replacement squadrons was one of the best things ever for naval aviation. The return on investment is tremendous. It is a little hard to measure and thus to convince

---

[*] The U.S. Navy began adding angled decks to its aircraft carriers in the 1950s to prevent landing aircraft that missed arresting wires from crashing into planes farther forward on the deck.

Congress of the worth of the RAGs, but they have held up under frequent review. At any rate, the majority of simulators are co-located with the RAGs for use in the replacement training syllabus.

Paul Stillwell: What did you do to coordinate the counterpart replacement squadrons on the two coasts, for a given airplane?

Admiral Osborn: I didn't have direct responsibility for that. The way it worked, and still works, is that one of the RAGs is designated the model manager for the aircraft. So that squadron is the granddaddy for the procedures process. Annually, a NATOPS conference is attended by the model manager, the other RAG for that aircraft, and representatives from the fleet. Any procedure that needs to be added or modified by virtue of fleet input is discussed and voted on. These changes then go out as a change to the manual.

Paul Stillwell: How much did you travel in that job?

Admiral Osborn: I was probably on each coast once every two or three months. The head of that division, OP-59, was Rear Admiral Fred Koch.[*] He was a very interesting man, so intelligent his mind would get ahead of his voice. He was very difficult to understand because he was thinking about two sentences ahead of what he was saying. It was a challenge to get the gist of what he was saying and understand what he wanted. I don't know why he took a liking to me, but he was the reason why I was selected one year early for O-6.[†] We were always good friends. Unfortunately, he passed away this last year.

Paul Stillwell: Could you carry the hierarchy up a little further then within the OP-05 organization?

---

[*] Rear Admiral Ferdinand P. Koch, USN, Director, Air Warfare Division, OpNav.
[†] O-6 is the pay grade for a Navy captain.

Admiral Osborn: Admiral Houser was OP-05 when I first got there, then Admiral Peterson and then Fox Turner.* Admiral Houser was distinguished in demeanor and appearance. Seemed to always be in control of himself and the situation. Of course, I didn't have much contact with him. I was in a meeting with him maybe once a week but never as a principal. He was impressive. This was the first time I had an opportunity to see the process of two- and three-stars working issues, the give and take, moving the issues through OpNav, OSD, and into the congressional process.† That was quite an awakening; it is for everybody.

Paul Stillwell: What kind of inputs can you offer on that process?

Admiral Osborn: It is sort of like a mouse trying to move an elephant down the road. I always was a bit frustrated with the process. It seemed to me like the OSD portion of the whole thing was not very effective, because the program sponsors and the Congress seemed to work around OSD. Maybe the process has changed since then. It is such a gargantuan system, and there are so many factors at play. Just within the E-ring, who is going to get the dollars amongst surface, air and submarines.‡ Within aviation, who is going to get the dollars amongst TacAir, VS, VP, and helicopters. By the time that all gets sorted out and turned over to OSD, nobody is happy with the compromise. When you get to Congress there are programs you don't want, and some that you want don't get funded because of where the contractors are located geographically. Today with very scarce resources, we can't afford that kind of waste. It is like bases. We have way too many air bases and Army posts. We can't close some of them because of their "congressional" location. That is not a good thing from the taxpayer standpoint.

---

* The following individuals served as OP-05, Deputy Chief of Naval Operations (Air Warfare): Vice Admiral William D. Houser, USN, 5 August 1972 to 30 April 1976; Vice Admiral Forrest S. Peterson, USN, 1 May 1976 to 5 October 1976; Vice Admiral Frederick C. Turner, USN, 6 October 1976 to 30 June 1979.
† OSD—Office of the Secretary of Defense.
‡ The Pentagon has lettered corridors, going from A at the innermost to E at the outermost. E-ring offices, which go around the perimeter of the building, are considered the most prestigious.

Paul Stillwell: I would say there has been considerable progress in recent years because of the procedures that have been put in.

Admiral Osborn: There is no question about it. However, since the last base closure process, the budget has closed down considerably, and we have more bases than we need. The chairman and service chiefs agree that we have bases out there that we can't afford or don't need. They would much rather have that money to put into training and parts and operating forces. The problem with physical plants is there must be constant money flowing in to keep them up. You get to the point where it is so costly to repair that it's not worth it. Thus, we have a lot of physical plants that are very, very run down. They haven't had progressive maintenance. At some point, some of those bases are going to have to be closed down. There doesn't seem to be much of another effort to get a BRAC going—for political reasons.*

Paul Stillwell: Before we started, you mentioned the business of parochialism in naval aviation. Do you want to address that at this point?

Admiral Osborn: I think we talked about that a little earlier. This tour that we are talking about now was where I was exposed to it in a programmatic sense. The hierarchy of naval aviation has historically been TacAir leadership, as it should be. That is the bulk of naval aviation. The problem is that TacAir aviators, from the bottom all the way to the top, have consistently put down patrol aviation in all their discussions; to almost the same degree, helicopters; and to lesser degree VS, simply because VS shares the carrier wardroom and has a tailhook. But still, there is tremendous parochialism and, in the competition for short budget dollars, decisions are based on what that leadership thinks is important. Which is probably okay, except that it is carried over into day-to-day interplay between individuals.

TacAir aviators constantly put down the other communities. This is counterproductive in a number of ways, and it certainly doesn't help on Capitol Hill. It is demoralizing to people who are not TacAir, because it shows itself in personnel issues

---

* BRAC—base realignment and closure.

and all kinds of ways. It decreases the overall effectiveness of naval aviation. This relationship has improved somewhat, but it will take a long time before it goes away. The only thing that will make it go away is technological advances and the way naval aviation is used in the bigger picture.

The platform in naval aviation will become less important than the weapons system and the sensors. That is evidenced a little bit by the way the P-3 is being used right now. The TacAir leadership recognizes today, much more than they ever have, the importance of patrol aviation—because of what the P-3 has been doing in the Adriatic. The missions the P-3 is doing in the Adriatic and elsewhere will continue to change all of that.[*]

The real issue that TacAir absolutely refuses to face is the business of a submarine attacking an aircraft carrier. Not since World War II has a carrier been attacked by an enemy. Carrier COs and flag officers aboard aircraft carriers have this false sense of well-being, because it has not happened in the last 50-plus years. It can, and possibly will, happen. The submarine threat is out there today. Maybe not from the Russians, but we have some pretty fancy diesel submarines sliding around the oceans. You have no idea who they belong to and may never know who fired that fateful torpedo that damaged or sunk that carrier. We have basically lost the integral ASW capability aboard carriers because of resources and training. The VS community has withered. The S-3 doesn't do ASW any more. They do logistics and tanking. Intentions are for the S-3 to disappear completely. This also raises a real issue of tanking capability for the air wing. The A-6 was a marginal tanker. The S-3 was an even less capable tanker. The F/A-18 doubling as a tanker will undermine operational readiness.[†] The last thing that you want is for the air wing to depend on the Air Force for fueling. That is fraught with all kinds of problems and serious implications.

---

[*] These new missions are discussed later in the interview.
[†] The F/A-18 Hornet, originally built by McDonnell Douglas, is a jet aircraft capable of both fighter and attack roles. It first entered operational service with VFA-125, a fleet readiness squadron, in May 1980. The F/A-18C model has a wingspan of 37 feet, 6 inches; length, 56 feet; gross weight of 36,710 pounds in the fighter version and 49,224 pounds in the attack version; top speed of 1,190 miles per hour. It replaced the F-4 Phantom and A-7 Corsair in fleet units.

Paul Stillwell: Of course, one of the big arguments for the carrier is that it can go places where you don't have land-based support.

Admiral Osborn: You have to hang your hat on that with the aircraft carrier, and it is a valid position. The carrier is one of our greatest assets in our defense posture.

Paul Stillwell: When you were in OP-05, did you see any personal evidence of this parochialism?

Admiral Osborn: You heard it in the hallways every day. It was there all the time. The thing you would hear over a beer and sometimes in the hallways was "VP pukes." Of course, that stems from the per diem issue. Per diem was the biggest rub of TacAir against VP, and for good reason. When I was WingsPac, I tried to get the whole per diem system changed because it was absolutely ludicrous. VP aircrews profit greatly from the per diem system. Air group personnel don't get a nickel. VP crews sit in a comfortable BOQ and a reasonably comfortable barracks and draw per diem. Per diem that allows you to cover the cost of living is one thing; per diem that allows you to put money in the bank is another thing. There are all kinds of places where the per diem rate is totally out of hand, and many places where VP shouldn't be getting per diem at all. But it is in the congressional language and very hard to change. It has done more damage than you can possibly imagine in terms of working together and mutual respect for each other.

Paul Stillwell: Isn't there also a little bit of a macho attitude that real men fly TacAir?

Admiral Osborn: Sure, there is a lot of that. And there is some good to it. Many VP aviators wanted to be TacAir aviators, and were good enough pilots, but the numbers didn't allow it. I was one of those guys. I wanted to fly single-engine AD Spads in the worst way and had the flight grades to support it. As I mentioned before, I got sidetracked by the numbers.

Paul Stillwell: We mentioned earlier that Captain Ed Martin was in OP-05 at that time as Admiral Houser's EA.[*] What do you remember of him?

Admiral Osborn: A very hard-working guy. I think he was still feeling some of the effects of his POW time.[†] Just a very evenhanded gentleman. Very impressive. He did a topnotch job as executive assistant—always approachable and always willing to help in any way.

Paul Stillwell: Are there any specific achievements that you would mark down for that period in OP-05 that you were able to bring about?

Admiral Osborn: I learned about this thing called Instructional Systems Development that some people were kicking around, where computers were used to develop self-paced learning firmware. So I looked into it. It sounded promising in terms of ground training for the fleet readiness squadrons. The process, now perfected to a great degree, was in its early stages. The student would start down through a series of written questions. Depending on how you answered the question, the system automatically takes you into another avenue. The student thus goes at his or her own pace. It might take one person three days to go through the maze, where another student might do it in an hour.

Paul Stillwell: Kind of an automated correspondence course.

Admiral Osborn: I rounded up a little money. In fact, Ed Waller got my first money for me.[‡] He was OP-951 at that time. I gave him a presentation, then asked him if he had a few bucks lying around to help me out. I think I asked him for $5,000, which he provided. It was some sweep-up money from somewhere. So we got that thing kicked

---

[*] Captain Edward H. Martin, USN, served in the 1970s as executive assistant to Admiral Houser and in the 1980s served as OP-05 himself. The oral history of Martin, who retired as a vice admiral, is in the Naval Institute collection.
[†] As Martin described in his oral history, he was a prisoner of war in Vietnam, from 1967 to 1973.
[‡] Rear Admiral Edward C. Waller III, USN, Commander Antisubmarine Warfare Systems Project Office.

off, and it was eventually implemented in all the RAGs. It worked pretty well and led to more sophisticated computer-based training. It saved a lot of training time.

Paul Stillwell: That's right, because the classroom has to go at more of a median pace, or even a little below that, to accommodate the slower people.

Admiral Osborn: While I was in that job, I was put in a nomination package for executive assistant (EA) to the Director of Antisubmarine Warfare and Ocean Surveillance (OP-095), which, at that time, was Vice Admiral Dan Murphy.[*] After being interviewed, I was selected for the job. Before I could report, Dan Murphy went to be the Deputy DCI at CIA.[†] Rear Admiral Frank McMullen, the deputy, had become acting 095 and was in the job when I reported in.[‡]

The word eventually came out that Vice Admiral Ed Waller was to be appointed the new 095. I didn't know where that left me, because I figured he probably had someone picked to be his executive assistant. I barely knew Waller. After thinking about it for a couple of days, I decided to go on the offense. So I called him and said, "I am going to be very straightforward on this, Admiral. I expect that you may have someone in mind as your EA, and I perfectly understand that. I think I can do the job well for you and would like to have a crack at it." I don't know whether that got me the job or not. We never discussed it after that. Anyway, he left me there. I think it worked out pretty well for both of us.

It was a shocking learning experience for me. Being an EA in the E-ring means that you are always behind. You are always ten steps behind what you should be doing, simply from the very heavy workload of the job. All the correspondence and paperwork flows through you to go to the principal. You have to try to make it good enough for him to see. So you end up either working with the originator to improve it or getting into a discussion with him about why it isn't good enough. It's a little nerve-racking at times. Anyone who has ever been in an EA job would agree.

---

[*] Vice Admiral Daniel J. Murphy, USN.
[†] DCI—Director of Central Intelligence; CIA—Central Intelligence Agency.
[‡] Rear Admiral Frank D. McMullen, Jr., USN, Deputy Director, Antisubmarine Warfare and Ocean Surveillance Programs.

Paul Stillwell: Did you have essentially a chief of staff role?

Admiral Osborn: I suppose you could say that. You control his time, his calendar. The aide kept his calendar, but as far as who saw him and when, it was your call. The other thing that makes the job interesting is that you have to kind of decide on your own whether you should sit in on the sessions in his office. The best thing would have been to sit in on all of them. Obviously, you can't, because you have to budget your time to keep the whole process going. The days are long in terms of time, but short in terms of getting everything done. I don't mind admitting that the job was getting to me after about three or four months. I was having real physical problems—tired all the time. Going home and wanting to go to bed immediately. I was getting up at 5:00 o'clock in the morning to be in the office by 6:00 or 6:30, then leaving the office at 6:30 or 7:00 in the evening after the principal went home.

Finally, I was really feeling poorly. I went to the flight surgeon at Andrews.[*] He checked me all over and then asked me to tell him about my work. It was obvious to him that I was doing this to myself. He said I had to get out of there occasionally, break up the routine. Admiral Waller understood. I told him my problem and that I had to do something about it. One of the things was to get away from the desk once in a while and try to go to the athletic center every day. He was all for that. He went down there every day. He spent longer periods down there than I did. He was very disciplined about his time. That was one of the things I admired about him. He made sure that he took time to sit and think about things, analyze issues—quiet time. That was a good learning experience for me, and I used it later to a degree. You can get a lot done in a half hour of quiet, uninterrupted time.

Paul Stillwell: What can you say about his personality?

---

[*] Andrews Air Force Base is located approximately ten miles southeast of Washington, D.C., in Prince George's County, Maryland.

Admiral Osborn: He was not easy to work for. He never spoke a harsh word to me. I'm not sure he ever corrected me in any way. I never knew if I was doing the job well or not. I never knew if I was irritating him. I could suspicion, but was never quite sure. The hardest thing, I was never sure whether I was putting myself in a place where he didn't want me. At the three-star level there are some very sensitive issues, sometimes at the personal level, sometimes sensitive from the classified need-to-know standpoint. Even though you may have all the clearance tickets, that doesn't necessarily mean that you should know everything about that subject. I had to make the calls on all that stuff. The day I left I didn't know whether I did a really good job, and still don't. I wouldn't say we are close, but over the years we have talked a lot. He and Marty have always been extremely nice to us and cordial.*

Paul Stillwell: One possible indication would be a fitness report. How did that go?

Admiral Osborn: The fitness reports were okay; otherwise I would not have made flag. His reports probably weighed heavily. I had a fitness report on my next job—now is probably as good a time as any to cover it. When I was the wing commander, my reporting senior had another wing commander and three station COs to compare on the same report, and I was ranked five of five. But I still made flag. Now, figure that one out. I don't think that has happened very often.

Paul Stillwell: That does say something about Admiral Waller's fitness reports.

Admiral Osborn: Fitness reports are only part of the picture at that level. There is a lot of verbal exchange amongst the decision-makers which weighs heavily.

Paul Stillwell: Did the physical regimen you went on help?

Admiral Osborn: Yes, it did. I also tried to relax a little bit more. It was probably a combination. I was beginning to get a better feel for the job, be more efficient. I should

---

* Marty is the nickname of Waller's wife Margaret.

have known; I should have remembered from when I was a squadron department head. I was one of the worst kind, trying to do everything myself because I thought I could do the job better than anyone else. Finally, I found that my officers could do the work well, sometimes better than I could have. Being an EA is a little bit different, because there is no one to delegate to. You have certain things to do as an EA, and nobody else could do them.

Paul Stillwell: What do you remember about the substance of the issues that paraded by you day by day?

Admiral Osborn: That was ASW and Ocean Surveillance. One of the big issues was a black program managed in 095, which we can't talk about here.[*] A multi, multi-million dollar program in aviation. It was under tremendous scrutiny by the CNO, OSD, and the Congress. Not under scrutiny by a large number of people because it was black. However, money was flowing into it at a fast rate. A civilian director under Admiral Waller was managing the program. He didn't feel that he needed anyone's help and played his cards pretty close to the belt. The admiral knew he had to be involved, so it was an interesting interaction between two people with big egos (any three-star has a big ego). Ocean surveillance from an overhead standpoint was becoming a major interest at the time, particularly what role, and how much of a role, imagery was to play.

Of course, the major thrust was ASW and how much of the budget pie it was going to have. That has always been a tough one because the program sponsors—aviation, surface and submarine—all dealt with that differently. The surface people were trying to get money for ships and towed arrays, which were just coming into operational capability.[†] Aviation was trying to build additional carriers and upgrade their TacAir platforms, along with other lesser but expensive programs. The submariners enjoyed a

---

[*] In this context a "black program" is one that is highly classified and thus not discussed in publicly available documents and records.
[†] A towed array consists of passive sonar sensors, as opposed to those mounted directly on the ship's hull. By being on a towline, the passive array has the advantage that it can be lowered through thermal layers that would otherwise inhibit sound propagation and reception.

"first among equals" status because of the strategic SSBN program and the clear need for more attack boats.

Paul Stillwell: Were you getting into the dedicated T-AGOS ships at that time?*

Admiral Osborn: Absolutely, OP-095 did have the money for the undersea surveillance system (IUSS). That was the operational program that 095 had the dollars for. The first T-AGOS ships were at sea at that time. So there were a lot of important things in the 095 division. Shortly after Admiral Waller took over, a budget division, OP-957, was formed. An O-6 was brought in as director and given the task of developing an ASW and Ocean Surveillance budget—but no money. The idea was that he was supposed to work with the program sponsors: air, surface and submarine. He could develop budgets all day long, but they didn't mean a thing when it came to the CEB's and final decision point about who was going to get what money.†

Paul Stillwell: Was this money supposed to be carved out of the barons' share?‡

Admiral Osborn: The budget he set up was supposed to be honored out of their money. ASW and Ocean Surveillance would be funded at X level with Y dollars, and the OP-05 portion would come from OP-05 dollars and so on. The barons had to play to it and recognize it, but when it all came to pass they didn't do a thing about it directly. That idea didn't work very well and went away after a few years.

Paul Stillwell: This must have been a very eye-opening tour for you on how the Navy at large works.

---

* T-AGOS is the designation for ocean surveillance ships operated by civil service mariners of the Military Sealift Command. They were equipped with the surveillance towed array sensor system (SURTASS), a submarine detection system.
† CEB—CNO Executive Board.
‡ In that period the Deputy Chiefs of Naval Operations for air, surface, and submarine warfare were known informally as the barons.

Admiral Osborn: Watching the way it worked between the CNO, VCNO, and three-stars was a very exciting time. Working with the other EAs to get things done was a good experience.

Paul Stillwell: Any of the other EAs that you remember specifically?

Admiral Osborn: Jim Service was the Vice Chief's EA at that time.[*] I worked closely with him. Tony Less was OP-05 EA part of the time.[†]

Paul Stillwell: You had mentioned Admiral Long earlier. Any comments on him?

Admiral Osborn: He was OP-02 at that time and later became VCNO.[‡] He and Waller got along very well, had many one-on-one sessions. I think that Long bounced ideas off Waller. They would often get together late in the afternoon and chat for an hour. The submarine community had tremendous respect for Long. He was a very effective OP-02. I don't know what Rickover thought of him.[§]

Paul Stillwell: I got the impression from interviewing Admiral Long that he was willing to stand up to Rickover.

Admiral Osborn: He certainly had the confidence to do that. I think he was probably able to say what he wanted to say to Rickover in a very quiet but effective way. My guess is that Rickover probably thought a lot of him.

---

[*] Captain James E. Service, USN, later a vice admiral.
[†] Captain Anthony A. Less, USN, later a vice admiral.
[‡] Vice Admiral Robert L. J. Long, USN, served as Deputy Chief of Naval Operations (Submarine Warfare) from September 1974 to July 1977. As a four-star admiral he was Vice Chief of Naval Operations from July 1977 to September 1979. His oral history is in the Naval Institute collection.
[§] Hyman G. Rickover was considered the father of the nuclear Navy. He ran the U.S. Navy's nuclear-power program for many years, from 1948 until he eventually left active duty in 1982 with the rank of four-star admiral on the retired list. Rickover Hall at the Naval Academy is named in his honor, as is the nuclear-powered attack submarine Hyman G. Rickover (SSN-709), which was commissioned 21 July 1984.

Paul Stillwell: Any observations on Admiral Holloway as CNO?[*]

Admiral Osborn: I didn't have that much contact with him, nor did I observe him a great deal. He commanded a lot of respect from the Chairman and Congress. He carried a lot of weight in Congress. He was good for the Navy and for aviation.

Paul Stillwell: Admiral Shear was VCNO for a while and he had been in that antisubmarine job.[†]

Admiral Osborn: He was Vice Chief when Waller was 095. I think that he reminded Admiral Waller more than once that he had just been 095. He was not one to let go of anything he knew about, and I think he felt ownership of 95 as Vice CNO. That may have caused a few problems. Again, Waller didn't share a lot of his thoughts with me, but I do remember him commenting a couple of times that he wished Shear would let go a little bit. I would monitor the Vice Chief's phone calls to Waller. A couple of them were quite interesting. He may have said, "I think you should do this" a couple of times in a fairly straightforward and blunt way.

Paul Stillwell: Any more specific issues that you want to mention?

Admiral Osborn: No, I don't think so.

Paul Stillwell: It must have been a very broadening tour in terms of your professional knowledge.

Admiral Osborn: Absolutely, the whole idea of how that process worked there in the E-ring is just remarkable. And how much the personnel issues came into play, the interplay between individuals. How much personalities affect decisions and the ability of

---

[*] Admiral James L. Holloway III, USN, served as Chief of Naval Operations from 29 June 1974 to 1 July 1978.
[†] Admiral Harold E. Shear, USN, served as Vice Chief of Naval Operations from 30 June 1975 to 5 July 1977. His oral history is in the Naval Institute collection.

people to work together. It is just there right on top of you all the time. Everything is kind of bare and laid out when you are in the midst of it.

Paul Stillwell: Any specific examples that you can mention of personalities affecting decisions?

Admiral Osborn: I really think that Admiral Shear tried to be a major decision-making force with the CNO and tried to push the three-stars in the direction he thought they ought to go. He kicked back a lot of decision papers to the three-stars, saying, "This is not going to work; you've got to do this a different way [other than it being resolved formally or informally in a somewhat collegial manner]." Admiral Ike Kidd was CinCLant at the time; Kelso was his EA.[*] Kidd carried a lot of sway in the E-ring. The force of his being was major in the E-ring when he was in Norfolk. There was an element of the geographic issue, i.e., that the Atlantic Fleet hierarchy plays a stronger role in Navy decision issues than the Pacific leadership.

Paul Stillwell: What manifestation did you see of this difference between the two fleets?

Admiral Osborn: I'm going to go back and answer an earlier question. Shear had it in his mind that whenever we were prosecuting a Soviet submarine, particularly an attack boat close off the coast, he, and the CNO by inference, should be kept up to date on what was happening in the prosecution. Of course, Ike Kidd was dead set against that, because this was interference with the role of the CinC. This came to a head two or three times. There was a compromise reached somewhere along the line. Someone at LantFlt headquarters would call Waller and kind of give daily updates. Waller would then tell Shear. But it was never going to be constant inputs into the CNO's command center.

---

[*] Admiral Isaac C. Kidd, Jr., USN, served as Supreme Allied Commander Atlantic, Commander in Chief Atlantic Command, and Commander in Chief Atlantic Fleet from 30 May 1975 to 30 September 1978. Captain Frank B. Kelso II, USN, later became a four-star admiral and served as Chief of Naval Operations from 1990 to 1994.

Paul Stillwell: By law the CNO is out of the CinCs' chain of command, but that didn't suit Shear's style.

Admiral Osborn: He didn't want to understand that.

Paul Stillwell: Within the limits of classification, how capable was the U.S. Navy in ASW in that era?

Admiral Osborn: Pretty capable. Of course, the IUSS, the SOSUS system, was the key to that. A tremendously successful program. And Blind Man's Bluff talked of the tapping into the Soviet communications link.[*] I think Waller may have known all about that, because once I read the book, a lot of things came back to me, little pieces of information that I had seen without having the whole picture.

Paul Stillwell: That is a remarkable book.

Admiral Osborn: I am not sure it served our best interests, but nevertheless it is out and is a remarkable book.

Paul Stillwell: One interest it served was for the submariners who had their achievements validated and recognized.

Admiral Osborn: I couldn't put it down. It was fun to read, because I knew some of those guys and recognized some of the incidents and prosecutions.

Back to the difference between the Atlantic and Pacific fleets. This is an interesting point that I expect you have heard many times before. The squeaky wheel gets the grease. The Atlantic Fleet is closer to the grease. LantFleeters spend more time talking to Washington and the Pentagon, both on the phone and in person. When the Pentagon has a question about how things are going or how they should go, nine times

---

[*] Sherry Sontag and Christopher Drew, with Annette Lawrence Drew, Blind Man's Bluff: the Untold Story of American Submarine Espionage (New York: Public Affairs, 1998).

out of ten they will turn to Lant for discussion and answers. The Atlantic Fleet is much more in the eyes of the Pentagon, OSD, and Congress than the Pacific Fleet. It's a geographical thing. The Pacific Fleet with its great expanse of ocean and Asian governments is not well understood in Washington. Also, the threat from across that pond called the Altlantic Ocean is much closer and more visible. Europe is close to our shore, and Washington is within military reach of potential unfriendly nations. The Pacific—being a gigantic body of water that doesn't even start till you get to California—has a tremendous psychological effect.

Paul Stillwell: It may be something as simple as being in the same time zone.

Admiral Osborn: There may be 20 factors, but the fact is, the good equipment goes to the Atlantic Fleet first. That is where all the attention is. It is the bane of PacFlt leadership in Makalapa.[*] It drives them crazy all the time because they can't get the attention of Washington. It's quite a phenomenon, and it has been there forever.

Paul Stillwell: What were the working hours in OP-95? Did that ever ease up?

Admiral Osborn: No, in order to have everything ready—intelligence brief and all that stuff—for the admiral when he came in about 7:30, I had to be there at 6:30. Which meant I had to leave my house about 5:45. He usually left about 6:25 in the evening, which meant I was out of there by 7:00 and home about 8:00 due to evening traffic. The nice thing about Waller was that he did not work Saturdays. I usually had to go in Saturday mornings to catch up. Most of the E-ring principals worked all day Saturday and sometimes Sunday.

[Interruption for lunch]

---

[*] Makalapa is the name of the area near Pearl Harbor on the island of Oahu, Hawaii, where Commander in Chief Pacific Fleet maintains his headquarters.

Paul Stillwell: At lunch you related a delightful story about Admiral Fluckey and Admiral Macpherson. I wonder if you could put that one on the record please.

Admiral Osborn: I was aide to Rear Admiral Macpherson, who was Commander ASW Group Five aboard USS Bennington. We were transiting to Tonkin Gulf with a stop in Pearl Harbor. Admiral Macpherson was a good friend of Rear Admiral Eugene Fluckey, ComSubPac.[*] They made contact, and Admiral Fluckey invited Macpherson to go to sea with him the next day aboard the USS Daniel Boone, an SSBN. I was invited to go along. We spent the day at sea with the two admirals in the wardroom talking and me listening, trying to remain unobtrusive while they told sea stories all day. It was quite an exciting experience, to say the least. Unfortunately, I don't remember any of the stories. Wish I had a tape recording. That would be wonderful. They were having a good time, knew each other well, and were totally relaxed. They talked about current issues also.

Paul Stillwell: After two tours in the Pentagon you went to Patrol Wing Five. It probably was a relief to get out of town.

Admiral Osborn: It was, and exciting to take command. I'll say that my most enjoyable time in the Navy was when I was in command. I really felt very much at home in command and was more relaxed in that capacity than anywhere else in the Navy. I was coming to the Atlantic Fleet for the first time which caught the attention of the people I was dealing with because there is, once again, a little parochialism among Atlantic Fleet people, feeling that they have a bigger picture in terms of Navy operations and tactics. It took a while for them to realize that I had some capability to deal with the issues. It was a wonderful tour.

However, the first thing that hit me when I checked on board was the gentleman I was relieving, Andy Wilkinson, telling me one of his squadrons was in a bad way.[†] They had lost an airplane on the Canary Islands when the navigation failed and they flew into a

---

[*] Rear Admiral Eugene B. Fluckey, USN, served as Commander Submarine Force Pacific Fleet from 1964 to 1966.
[†] Osborn relieved Captain Edward A. Wilkinson, Jr., USN, in June 1978.

mountain. Subsequent to the crash in March '78 they failed their NATOPS evaluation three times in a row. I was faced with a squadron that obviously had major deficiencies.

To determine the depth of the problem, I contacted the CO of the fleet readiness squadron, VP-30, in Jacksonville and asked if he would loan me some of his best people to do an inspection of the NATOPS program in the squadron. He sent a young lieutenant commander by the name of Dan Oliver (later vice admiral) and three others.[*] I briefed Dan on what the issue was and sent him over to the squadron. After the first day he came back and said "This is not a NATOPS problem; it is a leadership problem. There are leadership problems from top to bottom." He went on to say, "My first clue was when I was sitting in the wardroom with the squadron officers. When the squadron commanding officer came in, I was the only one that stood up." Really, what we had was a "McHale's Navy" of the highest order.

The squadron was about to go to South America to do UNITAS operations, so we had some fast work to do to get them ready to take the mission, which we were able to do.[†] The next two COs, being exceptionally fine leaders, turned the squadron around to a capable organization. Certainly, this situation pointed out that the leadership at the top and in the middle just didn't do their jobs, and it had devastating effects on the organization.

Paul Stillwell: How many squadrons did you have overall?

Admiral Osborn: Six squadrons, each with 9 airplanes and 12 crews and about 300 people. We were based at NAS Brunswick, Maine. The Brunswick squadrons, at that time, tended to deploy to Bermuda and Lajes.[‡] The Jacksonville squadrons deployed to Sigonella and Keflavik.[§]

---

[*] Lieutenant Commander Daniel T. Oliver, USN.
[†] UNITAS is the name given to a series of annual exercises in which U.S. Navy ships operate with those of South American navies.
[‡] Lajes do Pico is a town in the Azores Islands.
[§] Sigonella is in Sicily; Keflavik is in Iceland.

Paul Stillwell: Since you were based that far north, you needed some nice alternative deployment sites that were warmer.

How can you keep track of six squadrons? Certainly you are not physically present with them all the time.

Admiral Osborn: One of the things I did was not something that I hatched up; I just put a little more emphasis on it than others. I made what we called a retention visit to the deployed squadron at least once during their six months away. We looked at their retention programs, safety program, etc. I took a team of five or six people, and we did a semi-formal look at the squadron. I always felt like I had a pretty good feel of the health and welfare of the squadron. We were able to have a good feel of the squadrons at Brunswick through observation of their day-to-day operations. I took pretty much of a hands-off approach, but, at the same time, felt we had a good feel of the health of the squadrons. I placed major emphasis on safety. They knew this was the key thing. I flew with the crews frequently to see how they operated in the air. It seemed to work out quite well.

Paul Stillwell: Did you put any innovations in place during your time?

Admiral Osborn: Yes, when Waller was ComPatWingsPac, I was in one of the Moffett squadrons under his aegis.* He introduced a formal, and very structured, training syllabus for crew ASW training. This had never been done before in either fleet. It was an excellent program. He had developed the idea when he was CO of one of the first Navy P-3 squadrons. I saw how the program worked and observed how he did business. So when I got to this wing, I looked around the squadrons and found a sharp lieutenant commander that was about to detach. He came over to the wing; I threw some papers in front of him and told him how I wanted the program modified. I asked him if he knew where we were going. He said, "Absolutely, I think this is fantastic." So I gave him an office and said, "Put it together." We had it in print in about three weeks.

---

* ComPatWingsPac—Commander Patrol Wings Pacific Fleet.

Paul Stillwell: What modifications were needed to change it from Pacific to the Atlantic?

Admiral Osborn: Not a great deal. There were just some things I thought might work a little bit better, plus we tried to simplify it a little in a few places.

Paul Stillwell: What was the status of the anti-shipping mission at that time—equipping P-3s with Harpoons?[*]

Admiral Osborn: One of the squadrons in that wing, VP-23, fired the first operational Harpoon during my tenure. The CO of the squadron fired the first one, and then I fired the second.[†]

Paul Stillwell: Please describe that event.

Admiral Osborn: We were operating out of Puerto Rico. This was part of a large LantFlt exercise, and we had a good-sized target ship. This was totally new, so there was some apprehension at all levels. Actually, it turned out to be sort of anticlimactic. Everything went as advertised, we acquired the target on radar, set up the missile control system, and fired. When the missile goes, the plane jumps up just a little, then you see it streaking out toward the horizon until out of sight. The tactical coordinator has the control system at his station, and the firing button is in the flight station. The missile did its job and sank the ship. As I remember, it was about 40 miles away at the time of missile launch.

Paul Stillwell: Did new doctrine have to be written to cover that mission?

Admiral Osborn: Yes, most of that was done by VX-1 in conjunction with VP-23.[‡]

---

[*] Harpoon is an antiship missile with a range of approximately 75-80 nautical miles. It can be fired from surface ships, submarines, and aircraft. The first combat use of Harpoon was against Libyan missile craft in the Gulf of Sidra in 1986.

[†] On 18 July 1979 Patrol Squadron 23 became the first Navy patrol squadron to fire the new Harpoon AGM-84 air-launching antiship missile. VP-23 was also the first fleet squadron to make an operational deployment with Harpoon. Commander Henry H. Davis, Jr., USN, commanded VP-23 from 20 October 1978 to 8 November 1979.

[‡] VX-1—Air Experimental and Development Squadron One.

Paul Stillwell: Was over-the-horizon targeting a concern in that?

Admiral Osborn: Not for that particular event, because we had enough altitude to have good radar coverage of the target and surrounding area. In fact, before the first missile was fired the area became "fouled" because of a non-exercise target straying into the area. I think we were using about 30 miles of clear area around the target.

Paul Stillwell: Over-the-horizon can be a concern. I remember in the Falklands the Argentineans were firing Exocet missiles, and I think at one point they were trying to hit a combatant and hit the Atlantic Conveyer instead because that was the first big ship it homed in on. Have any of the other missions changed at all since you had command of the squadron?

Admiral Osborn: Yes, it has changed tremendously, and this alludes back to what we were talking about earlier—the kinds of things the P-3 is doing now in the Adriatic, over-land, long-distance photography and infrared detection of land movements. The sensing equipment is all new. The mission of the P-3 has evolved considerably toward battle group protection and over-land work with less emphasis on ASW.

Paul Stillwell: Was it almost totally an ASW weapons system at the time you commanded the wing?

Admiral Osborn: ASW and ocean surveillance. When I say ocean surveillance, this has been a historic mission to look at what is on the surface of the water, shipping of all kinds and general surveillance of the ocean area for intelligence purposes. This has now been modified considerably by the addition of these other missions.

Paul Stillwell: One thing I have heard from talking to unit commanders is there is a little sense of frustration that they don't have as much hands-on control as when they were commanding officers. Did you find any of that phenomenon?

Admiral Osborn: Yes, but it didn't bother me too much. I flew enough with the squadrons to feel a part of the process and had enough contact with the COs, in a hands-off way, that I really felt a part of all the squadrons. That really never became anything of importance to me.

Paul Stillwell: And it's really not comparable to being in a ship where you are literally not allowed to give rudder orders. Any specific squadrons or squadron skippers that you want to recall?

Admiral Osborn: Certainly the one who was commanding officer of the squadron that had the problem I mentioned earlier. As an aside, I took over, and he was due to be relieved in due course in five or six days. When I got the full picture of what was going on in the squadron, I went to my senior, who was Dick Hedges and requested permission to fire him before the change of command because I wanted to make an issue of it.[*] It was a harsh action, but I felt the problem was severe enough in the squadron that it was justified, that he rated being made an example of, and that it would do a lot of good in the future if he did get relieved early. Hedges wouldn't go along with it.

Paul Stillwell: What can you say about your relationship with Admiral Hedges?

Admiral Osborn: Not very good. I didn't respect him a great deal. I didn't think he had what it took to do the job.

Paul Stillwell: Any specifics you want to mention?

Admiral Osborn: I always felt like he was a figurehead to a degree. He was very oriented to how he personally looked in the eyes of others, that he showed well. In fact, this thing I just mentioned is an example. Don't make any waves. Don't rock the boat.

---

[*] Rear Admiral Ralph R. Hedges, USN, Commander Patrol Wings Atlantic Fleet.

Paul Stillwell: You and he had completely opposite agendas on that point.

Admiral Osborn: Absolutely. You may remember, earlier in the interview I went through the issue of the plane commander who lied to me about a flight situation. I removed him from flight status and gave him a naval aviator evaluation board. That did more good for squadron safety then, and I'm sure after that, than anything else I could have done. Those people knew I was serious about squadron safety. I drew on that experience in deciding to take this drastic action of firing a commanding officer.

Paul Stillwell: Since you were frustrated in that, did you find another way to send the message?

Admiral Osborn: Yes, in terms of the amount of emphasis I put on safety from that time on. I had frequent discussion with the COs as a group, using that issue as an example. I certainly never told them that I wanted to fire the CO, but the point was made.

Paul Stillwell: And the loss of a patrol plane gave you a specific case to point to on the need for safety. How much administrative requirement was on you in that job?

Admiral Osborn: Not very much. I was blessed with an administrative officer that I could rely on 100% to have things absolutely perfect. His name was John Ryan.[*]

Paul Stillwell: Is there any connection between his now being superintendent and your son being flag secretary?[†]

Admiral Osborn: I don't think so. When Tom got ready to transfer, he knew this job was open and asked to be considered. He got the job, but I don't have any idea what the process was. Maybe a little bit below the surface, but not likely.

---

[*] Lieutenant Commander John R. Ryan, USN.
[†] As a vice admiral, Ryan became superintendent of the Naval Academy on 4 June 1978 and was in that billet at the time of this interview.

Paul Stillwell: What do you remember of John Ryan from 20 years ago?

Admiral Osborn: An absolute professional. Very in tune with the issues. Very smooth in his dealings with other people. No question, even at that time, he was on top of things. He made very clear what his position was, and he expected excellence around him. Very politically astute, which is no doubt serving him well in his current job. Just an all-around outstanding officer and leader.

Paul Stillwell: Any specific events or incidents you remember about him back then.

Admiral Osborn: He remembers one and reminds me of it every time we talk, it seems like. One of our squadrons had won an award, or just returned from deployment. He wrote a congratulatory message and sent it out in my absence. The only trouble was that it was sent to the wrong squadron.

Paul Stillwell: It is gracious of you that he is the one who remembers it rather than you.

Admiral Osborn: I don't think they could have picked a better person for here. You know, he did wonderful things over in Naples.* He was really responsible for closing down the old facility and all the construction of the new facility. At that time, Admiral Lopez was over there as CinCSouth.† Our other Navy son was his aide. When we went to Naples, Admiral Lopez told me that John Ryan was absolutely the best thing he had ever seen happen.

Paul Stillwell: What was Brunswick like as a place to live and operate from?

---

* As a rear admiral Ryan served as Commander Maritime Surveillance and Reconnaissance Force, U.S. Sixth Fleet/Commander, Fleet Air Mediterranean/Commander Maritime Air Forces, Mediterranean from September 1995 to May 1998.
† Admiral T. Joseph Lopez, USN, served as Commander in Chief U.S. Naval Forces Europe/Commander in Chief Allied Forces Southern Europe from October 1996 to October 1998.

Admiral Osborn: It is very nice. Sometimes people don't want to go there, because they think it is so cold. Once they get there, they don't want to leave. It is not a highly populated area. The fishing is great. As far as operating aircraft, it isn't so nice in the winter. Snow and ice can become a real problem and challenge. The first year we were there we got 60-plus inches of snow in the month of January. That wouldn't be bad by itself, because the snow removal equipment was excellent, but it would snow, then melt, then freeze. This left ice, sometimes furrows of ice, on the parking ramps. This made it very difficult to walk or move planes on the ramp. Then it would snow on top of the ice with the melting and freezing all over again. These come-and-go snowstorms, with a couple of Indian summers mixed in, resulted in the worst possible conditions to operate aircraft.

Paul Stillwell: How do you stop when you put your brakes on and try to land?

Admiral Osborn: Seldom was the runway not useable and safe. If a runway is plowed off and there is a couple or three inches of snow, that is not a bad surface to operate on. The P-3 happens to be a very good aircraft to operate on ice and snow, because four turboprop engines provide excellent directional control, even with crosswind. With regard to ice, at Brunswick they used a urea mixture which would melt the ice even under cold conditions. The real problem is on the ramps, trying to walk and move planes in the cold and wind. It's not much fun and very treacherous. Those same conditions persist at Keflavik and in Alaska.

Paul Stillwell: Did planes from your wing have any notable successes against Soviet submarines during that period?

Admiral Osborn: Yes, we had a number of successful missions in the Mediterranean with deployed squadrons. The Soviets were operating heavily in the Med at that time, and we had a number of very successful prosecutions. Out of Keflavik we were keeping track of the SSBNs on a regular basis and doing a good job of keeping hold of them.

Paul Stillwell: How does interoperability work in that situation? You are trying to gather the VP, SOSUS, towed arrays, and other sources.

Admiral Osborn: The VP and SOSUS interoperability was finely tuned as a result of years of growing up together. The SOSUS system was a way to cue VP to the target, so the two were tied together from the start. Procedures were built for the two systems to support each other. With respect to frigates with towed arrays, there really weren't a whole lot of times when the three systems could do operational missions together. As far as the IUSS towed arrays, the T-AGOS ships, the bulk of that capability came on after I was with the wing. The T-AGOS contact information was piped to the IUSS center in Norfolk, just as the fixed-array information was, so the initial source didn't make any difference. It came from the system.

Paul Stillwell: So Norfolk would handle it even for things in the Med?

Admiral Osborn: The system didn't reach into the Med. Certainly there was towed-array work that went on in the Med, and was tied in through the command structure of Sixth Fleet. There were a number of good exercises and operations with frigate towed arrays in the Med. It was a good environment and where early operational testing was done.

Paul Stillwell: Admiral Train told me that when he was Sixth Fleet one of the missions Admiral Holloway assigned him was to work with the towed array.[*] A dramatic incident took place in which a Soviet Echo II collided with the USS Voge. Anything else to mention on Patrol Wing Five?

Admiral Osborn: I don't think so.

Paul Stillwell: Back to Washington again and Naval Military Personnel Command. What did your job involve there?

---

[*] Vice Admiral Harry D. Train II, USN, commanded the Sixth Fleet from 5 August 1976 to 1 September 1978. The oral history of Train, who retired as a four-star admiral, is in the Naval Institute collection.

Admiral Osborn: My title was Director, Restricted Line and Staff Placement. Now, what that means—my division was responsible for filling billets for doctors, dentists, lawyers, supply corps, engineers, chaplains, public affairs, and intelligence. We also filled all personal staff billets of flag officers. It was a very interesting job and one where I learned a great deal about the other parts of the Navy.

Paul Stillwell: Was this a direct payback for your postgraduate work?

Admiral Osborn: On purpose or accidental. Sometimes I thought it was accidental when compared with how the Navy used their postgraduate investment. To be charitable, yes, that was my payback tour.

Paul Stillwell: Did you find the postgraduate education beneficial in this tour?

Admiral Osborn: Yes, but certainly not necessary. My education in Monterey was personnel management, but there wasn't any one course that helped at NMPC. I guess the thing I brought from Monterey that helped was the general organizational management skills we worked on at postgraduate school.

Paul Stillwell: You said you learned a lot in that job. What were some of the things you learned?

Admiral Osborn: The restricted line components are organizations unto themselves.[*]

Paul Stillwell: Each of those components has its own "pope," if you want to call it that.

Admiral Osborn: Absolutely, the doctors and dentists don't want to have any help or interference from anybody else. The lawyers want to run their own entity. None of these restricted line and staff components want help from the greater Navy, and this can be

---
[*] These components are the naval aviators, submariners, and surface warfare officers.

very counterproductive. The reason this is dangerous is because they get out of tune with the line Navy. You saw how many times the medical department got off track by not following the basic leadership and management procedures that have been time tested in the Navy forever. One of the biggest travesties I saw in the Medical Corps was the lack of leadership ability among their people. The doctors and dentists didn't want to think about leadership and dealt with enlisted personnel on a first-name basis. It took away from their readiness significantly.

Paul Stillwell: Navy medicine got a tremendous black eye in the 1980s from malpractice—call it what you want, a lot of problems.[*]

Admiral Osborn: You can't take a lot of time sending doctors to long schools to teach leadership, but there wasn't enough emphasis put on the leadership aspects of being an officer. The business I mentioned before of doctors and dentists being on a first-name basis with their enlisted personnel and socializing with them and those kinds of things. Our Navy has been going for many years, and these ways of doing business have been put in place for good reasons; they are tried and true. Those things were ignored at cost to them. I never had any trouble dealing with those various components, but I got the message really clear, "Don't push too hard into our bailiwick, because all we want you to do is help us get the right people into our billets. Don't make too many waves."

Paul Stillwell: How did the process work out in practice? How was detailing handled?

Admiral Osborn: The doctors had their own detailer, for example. My division was responsible for moving the people involved in a billet change in accordance with their detailer's plan, but keeping the whole process within the Navy personnel system. Each of

---

[*] During the mid-1980s the Navy's Medical Corps was beset by charges of negligence, incompetence, and malpractice. See Arthur M. Smith, "Are We Losing Confidence in Navy Medicine?" U.S. Naval Institute Proceedings, May 1986, pages 120-131.

those components moved the people they wanted to move, but that had to fit into the proper process.

Paul Stillwell: What part of the process did your people do? How did you take the desires from that particular community and fit it in the larger whole?

Admiral Osborn: It would be most accurate to say that it was largely an oversight responsibility. The process really took place with what the detailer did, and we oversaw that to make sure the action was done in accordance with established personnel policy and procedures. Policy dictated a number of requirements that had to be met for a set of transfer orders to be appropriate. People could not be moved capriciously or indiscriminately for someone's personal agenda, which can happen very easily if not monitored. Personnel detailing is fraught with opportunity for someone to do a favor for someone else, or get even for something in the past. There are all kinds of things that can take place, and do, if you don't have systematic oversight and management.

Paul Stillwell: Did you have the ability that if you saw something outrageous to step in?

Admiral Osborn: Yes, that happened sometimes. Of course, I had the backing of my boss, the Director of Personnel Distribution. At that time it was Admiral Pete Conrad.[*] Anything that was not working right and I needed his help, he was there and backed me 100%. He was a wonderful man to work for.

Paul Stillwell: Did you have cases where you overturned placements that had been decided on?

Admiral Osborn: I did change doctor details a few times. Lawyers—I don't think there was ever a need to take any action with regard to what they had going. We had to keep an eye on the supply officers. They wanted to do a few things that were a little too

---

[*] Rear Admiral Peter C. Conrad, USN, Assistant Commander for Personnel Distribution, Naval Military Personnel Command.

smooth. It was generally somebody wanting to claim a hardship, or, at that time there were beginning to be decisions regarding husband-and-wife teams. Trying to get husband-and-wife teams moved to a certain spot where it was not detrimental to the Navy—a place where there was a meaningful billet for both members. We plowed some new ground in that area.

The next job I went to was up the line as deputy for that same division. There we were beginning to deal with a lot of single-parent issues, including written commitments by single parents stating that there was going to be someone to take care of their dependents when they deployed or went to sea. Going back to the restricted line and staff, there were occasional cases where an individual had convinced the detailer that he or she should be moved to a certain place for the following personal reasons with no documentation or formal hardship proceedings taking place—those kinds of things.

Paul Stillwell: I would guess that the detailing of couples was even more difficult if one of the pair was married to someone of a service other than the Navy.

Admiral Osborn: Really, at that time our position was that accommodation in that situation was almost a "too hard." If that person wanted to stay in the Navy, they needed to go where we wanted to send them. My guess is that the whole process has gotten harder and harder. The Navy is so much more attuned to the needs of single parents and husband/wife teams than we used to be.

Paul Stillwell: Even the business of allowing a mother to stay on active duty was a change. Sometime before that, ten years or so, Admiral Zumwalt had made the push to give greater opportunity to blacks and other minorities. What effect did you see of that by this time?

Admiral Osborn: I saw us bending over backwards in the personnel business to implement that policy. Doing some things we really didn't want to do in order to make it happen. Putting people in places they should really have never gone to meet those requirements. They weren't qualified, or the job was more than they could handle. Of course, nearly every time when they got to the job, the issue became larger, because they were frustrated and their senior was frustrated because they weren't doing the job. This was no fault of the individual. They had been put in a position that they didn't fit. This "forced fit" didn't happen a lot, but it did happen.

Paul Stillwell: Did you have any cases where the individual rose to the challenge?

Admiral Osborn: Oh, sure, and that has to be considered any time you talk about this. There were cases where I wanted to bet it wasn't going to be successful, and it worked out fine.

Paul Stillwell: Do you have any idea what the batting average was in that regard?

Admiral Osborn: No, I don't. When I was commanding officer of a squadron, we had a black officer who was not a very good pilot. He didn't have the motor skills to be a good pilot. We did everything we could think of, and more, to try to get him through the training syllabus. If he had been white, we would have held a Field Naval Aviator Evaluation Board on him, and he would probably have lost his wings. As it was, we stuck with him. My guess is that he was never put in the position of being in command of an airplane, flew copilot most of the time, and never had a clear flight responsibility. Again, not his fault. He had been passed along through the system and given a marginal okay at critical points.

Paul Stillwell: Where was the direction coming from to bend over backward, as you put it?

Admiral Osborn: From the CNO. There was a lot in writing that we had to lean to the benefit of the doubt, and the numbers had to improve.

Paul Stillwell: That was also the era of a great deal of concern about drugs in the Navy. Probably that wouldn't impact at the level you were dealing with to the extent it would with enlisted personnel.

Admiral Osborn: No, I was more involved with that in the next job as deputy to the director of personnel distribution, and then as head of personnel distribution. It was about that time that the Navy was in the first iteration of a solid drug policy. Testing was becoming sophisticated so you could really present solid evidence. Early drug testing was fairly problematical for a number of reasons, not the least of which was mistakes in the medical department with the tests. Results were unreliable for a while. About the time I was there in the personnel business, drug testing had become pretty solid.

Paul Stillwell: What was your relationship with the manpower people? Did you have any effect on billet levels and where they would be assigned—how many doctors, how many lawyers?

Admiral Osborn: That was pretty well handled on the OP-01 manpower side.[*] But we worked back and forth and frequently worked things out. The billet people needed to know from the detailers and placement people where reality fit with their wishes—supply and demand. We worked closely with them all the time. The "doers" (detailers) didn't have direct control over changing billets.

Paul Stillwell: Whose responsibility was it to ensure that there was an adequate supply to meet that billet level?

Admiral Osborn: It started with OP-01 stating the requirement, then the recruiting command filling those requirements into the training commands. The detailers take the inventory and try to spread it with priorities. Priorities were a big issue, because there were never enough people to fill all the billets. Priorities changed depending on a lot of

---

[*] OP-01—Deputy Chief of Naval Operations (Manpower, Personnel, and Training).

factors. That is where the coordination took place between the detailing side and the personnel requirement side.

Paul Stillwell: You talked mostly about the staff corps. What do you remember about the restricted line communities?

Admiral Osborn: I was very impressed with the engineers. They ran a good show and policed themselves well. Seldom did we have to recommend any change. It wasn't, "You will do this," but more like, "You probably need to take another look at this." Issues seldom came up with the engineers. Not only was I impressed with their top personnel man, who usually went on to be a flag officer, but also, the top-level people. It always seemed like they were part of the Navy. I didn't always feel that way about the doctors and dentists. The supply folks did a pretty good job.

Paul Stillwell: How about some of the esoteric ones like cryptography and public affairs?

Admiral Osborn: Public affairs is another issue. I don't think public affairs got very good quality people. They needed more quality. I did not have a great deal of respect for the Chief of Information at any time that I was in the Navy. That may be saying there is a media bias. As a general rule, it didn't seem like you could count on the Navy to handle a media issue in a professional way. That is not always the Chief of Information's problem. He may be echoing what the CNO wants to do, but too many times we have dealt with things by trying to keep information from the media, and to partially cover up by saying something was something it wasn't. Almost always, the true picture comes out. You end up swallowing your words, and the Navy looks bad. In most cases, except where national security is involved, you are better off giving as much straight information as you can, as soon as you get it. Tailhook was a public relations total disaster. It was a total disaster from start to finish, but certainly a public relations disaster. I am probably generalizing too much, but it didn't seem that we had well-trained, sharp people making the decisions in the Chinfo area.

Paul Stillwell: You would describe them as having a lower level of professionalism than the engineers.

Admiral Osborn: Certainly. I felt that the sharpest, most well rounded people in the Navy were the intelligence community. It is almost a toss-up in my view between them and the submariners. These two communities stand heads and shoulders above the other communities in terms of professionalism and broad understanding of the big picture. I say this overall for the intelligence community. The submariners don't necessarily have an edge on the big picture, but they stand out in technical professionalism.

Paul Stillwell: That is a legacy from Admiral Rickover.

Admiral Osborn: Absolutely. No compromise in technical professionalism. That is what the other communities should have. For one reason, the accident rate is directly affected by technical professionalism. There are all kinds of reasons why you should operate that way, but certainly the accident rate is reason enough.

Paul Stillwell: Anything else you would like to offer on that tour.

Admiral Osborn: One story. The commandant of midshipmen at the Naval Academy was due to be filled. Me being a naive guy in this restricted line and staff placement job, I went about filling it like I did the all the other key flag staff billets. That meant putting together a package of three or four likely candidates with their credentials. Somehow, Admiral Lawrence, Superintendent of the Naval Academy, got wind of this and called me.* He said, "Oak, I understand you are working on the new commandant." I said that I was, whereupon he said, "Let me save you a lot of time and effort. You don't need to do that. That job is none of your concern. I'll take care of it myself!" So that was the end of that.

---

* Vice Admiral William P. Lawrence, USN, served as Superintendent of the Naval Academy from August 1978 to August 1981. His oral history is in the Naval Institute collection.

Paul Stillwell: Was he circumventing the procedures?

Admiral Osborn: No, he was saying it was a unique job, that it was going to be Naval Academy graduate, and, "We know all the Naval Academy graduates like the back of our hand. We know which are logical candidates, and we are going to pick him over here." In actuality, he and his staff picked one and got the CNO's okay.*

Paul Stillwell: It is sort of analogous to these other communities picking their own people.

Admiral Osborn: There is another little thing about that job. I had someone on my staff who was a unique and famous person. Her name was Fran Galbraith. She was civilian and my assistant for flag staff detailing. She made initial selection of candidates that might fit an aide or flag secretary job. She had been in that job so long that every flag officer knew her by first name. She was so good that she could do the placement job for these people with very little help. I knew what was going on all the time and what she was doing, but she had such a sense of the kind of person required that almost every time picked a good fit. She was the in the job for 20 or 25 years and just retired a couple years ago. If you were to ask any of the four stars who Fran Galbraith was, they would talk to you at length about her superb ability.

Moving on to the next job, I just stepped up one notch in NMPC and became the deputy director of the whole Navy personnel distribution system, the detailing of all officer and enlisted personnel. My boss was Rear Admiral Pete Conrad, and later Al Herberger.† Basically, I oversaw the day-to-day administration of the division. The hard ones that nobody could solve found their way to my desk, the individual cases.

---

* Captain Leon A. "Bud" Edney, USN, served from 1981 to 1984 as the Naval Academy's commandant of midshipmen. He subsequently became a four-star admiral. His final active duty billet was as Supreme Allied Commander Atlantic and Commander in Chief Atlantic Command, 18 May 1990 to 13 July 1992.
† Rear Admiral Albert J. Herberger, USN.

Paul Stillwell: What would be some examples of hard ones?

Admiral Osborn: Contested hardship cases. Congressman A calling, or writing, and saying that he couldn't understand why Airman First Class Jones was going to station X when his qualifications were better for some other place, often near the petty officer's home. Congressman B asking about one of his constituents that had just been dropped out of flight training for poor flight grades and not understanding how that could happen. These were the kind of things that no one at a lower level was going to decide on without kicking them upstairs.

Paul Stillwell: How much sway did the congressmen have in getting those things changed?

Admiral Osborn: Not very much generally. Really the only time was when there were facts we did not know about. It didn't happen very often. In general, the Navy hierarchy holds pretty steady on things like that. There is a rare occasion where a powerful congressman can get something changed that should not be, but not often.

Paul Stillwell: There was a case such as that where Admiral Stan Arthur was derailed from being CinCPac.* The standard case is probably when you give the congressman the facts, who in turn relays them to the complaining parents, and that is the end of it.

Admiral Osborn: The other thing that happens is where one of the staffers signs a letter out on behalf of the congressman. The congressman might not have written the letter in the first place if it had been brought to his attention. That happens more often than not.

---

* On 26 June 1994 the Department of Defense withdrew the nomination of the Vice Chief of Naval Operations, Admiral Stanley R. Arthur, USN, who had been slated to serve as Commander in Chief Pacific. There was a concern that his Senate confirmation would be a protracted one at a time of increasing tensions in Korea. Senator David Durenberger (Republican-Minnesota) had placed a hold on the nomination to pressure the Navy for information on the case of Lieutenant Rebecca Hansen. Durenberger expressed concern that Hansen had been washed out of helicopter flight training as retaliation for charging sexual harassment on the part of an instructor. Admiral Jeremy M. Boorda, USN, Chief of Naval Operations at the time, was heavily criticized for not having given Admiral Arthur stronger backing. Boorda later said that his failure to be more supportive was the biggest regret of his tenure as CNO.

And it happens more than it used to because the staffers do so much more of some congressmen's work. Many of those staffers don't have the foggiest idea of what the system is, how it works, the criteria for decision. Nine times out of ten it will go away when you explain the facts and process to them. If this case is the son of someone that has been pumping money to Senator Stennis for years, it is not going to go away easily.[*]

Paul Stillwell: How did you deal with cases like that?

Admiral Osborn: If it hangs in, after some back and forth communication, then the CNO eventually gets involved.

Paul Stillwell: Was your job mainly dealing with these fire drills and exceptions to the norm?

Admiral Osborn: No, there was some policy development and dealing with policy issues with the heads of the warfare detailing branches. Ron Eytchison, later a rear admiral, was the submarine detailer when I was in that job.[†] Ben Cloud was the aviation detailer.[‡] Dick Ustick, later a rear admiral, was the surface detailer.[§]

I wasn't in that deputy job very long due to a couple of factors. First, I went into Bethesda Naval Hospital for hip surgery and not long after was selected for flag. The hardest part of that job was getting to work. I was barely ambulatory and on crutches for months, most of it wintertime. Trying to get into a vehicle, get to work, and up stairs to my office to get propped up at my desk was by far the hardest part of the day.

Paul Stillwell: You told me the story earlier when we were not recording. Can you relate it again?

---

[*] John C. Stennis (1901-1995) was a Democrat from Mississippi. He was in the U.S. Senate from 1947 to 1989, including service as chairman of the Armed Services Committee. The aircraft carrier John C. Stennis (CVN-74) is named in his honor.
[†] Captain Ronald M. Eytchison, USN.
[‡] Captain Benjamin W. Cloud, USN.
[§] Captain Richard C. Ustick, USN.

Admiral Osborn: I was jogging in those days and got to where I could not run anymore. The orthopedic surgeons at Bethesda said I had arthritis in my hip joint. They gave the choice of hip replacement or a procedure called osteotomy. I elected the osteotomy, which meant cutting through my hipbone and changing the angle of the ball of my hip in the joint. During the course of the operation, anything that could go wrong did, with a lot of permanent damage. I spent a month in the hospital and a month at home in bed. It was a bad experience and had a real impact on my ability to do the job. At about the same time I was selected for flag, Al Herberger received orders, so I was moved up to take his position as the director of distribution. It was nearly the same job as deputy, except the buck stopped at the director desk more often. Rear Admiral Bob Dunn was the commander of Naval Personnel Command and my boss.*

Paul Stillwell: Just to go back a little, you said you had some policy issues when you were in the deputy job. What were included in those?

Admiral Osborn: Length of tours, how to do the detailing process; how much time to put in orders for pre-schools, leave time. Mostly process. Let's take the case of an officer from the time the billet needs to be filled, how the detailer goes about selecting the individual, verbal communication with the primary candidate. Dealing with constituents was always a big issue. Discussion with an individual about his or her next duty station is a very personal and emotional process. Policy on how to do that in a positive manner was one of the most important aspects.

There were two things that came out strongly when I was the director. First was the politics. An officer or enlisted person may have worked for an admiral a few years back, and that admiral now wants the individual to go to such and such a billet. It may not be a fit, or it may not be possible, but he wants it to happen. Or he may want a certain person to come to work for him. Even more difficult is when a very senior officer weighs in on behalf of a constituent that is involved in a problem.

---

* Rear Admiral Robert F. Dunn, USN. The oral history of Dunn, who retired as a vice admiral, is in the Naval Institute collection.

The second thing I saw was how careful you have to be in oversight of detailers and how they conduct themselves in the job. For some reason, there is always a small percentage of detailers who envision themselves as God when it comes to assignment of people in their area of jurisdiction. They tend to deal with the individual as a policeman, rather than someone who should be helping them get assigned to the right place—shoving things down their throats, so to speak. A fair amount of counseling is involved. On a number of occasions it was necessary to call in the head of a detailing branch and request that he correct this kind of a problem with one of his detailers. Of course, the reason I would know about it was that the person being mistreated would tell his or her boss, who would call me or my deputy. More often than not, it was the personality of the detailer. It wasn't his intent to do it the wrong way, but rather his overbearing personality. Occasionally it was necessary to move that person out of the detailing business.

Paul Stillwell: Fitness reports must be the bread and butter in making a lot of these assignments. What can you say about the constant complaint about grade inflation on fitness reports?

Admiral Osborn: We are going back to the iteration before the one we have now, that is, the one the current one Admiral Boorda instituted when he became CNO. He felt like there was a major problem with inflation. Unfortunately, from looking at this new report form and talking to several officers who have used it, and others who have received it as a report of their fitness, it wasn't a very successful change. I believe it is fair to say, the Navy is using a fitness report system that isn't the best. It is very restrictive in terms of breaking out one person from another. It is very hard to do that with the current system. Now, going back to the previous system, which was in effect for many of my senior years, there was blatant inflation. Specifically, a reporting senior might rate three or four different officers who were peers as number one of ten (or whatever the total number of peers).

By the same token, I never felt it created a big problem. You could usually tell the facts. When you have a person's full package of fitness reports and you have a selection board, nine times out of ten you can figure out what the real picture of that officer is. I don't think that inflation ever created a big problem in the selection process. The system did need to be revised, but the result isn't quite what was intended. The design of the current fitness reporting form does not allow the reporting senior of two absolutely superb officers to show they are both equally worthy of command. This becomes a problem when there is a very limited number of command billets, as there is today.

Paul Stillwell: In your own case you mentioned being ranked five of five and still making flag rank. Do you think there was a perception that there was some kind of animosity between you and Admiral Hedges that people were taking into consideration.

Admiral Osborn: I'm sure there was.

Paul Stillwell: Describe your reaction when you found out you had been selected.

Admiral Osborn: Being in NMPC, I had all these old flag writers working for me who were now warrant officers or LDOs.* There is a Washington "underground" of former flag writers, now officers, that won't quit. These guys and gals are on the phone all the time talking to each other, and they think they have the inside scoop on everything happening at the highest levels of the Navy. That is true about 50% of the time! My LDO called me at home the night the flag list was about to come out. He said he had just talked to someone who had seen the final list, and I was not on it. About an hour later we were at a party at a neighbor's house when I got a call. It was my boss, Admiral Herberger. He told me that I had been selected. That was quite a thrill.

Paul Stillwell: Would you describe it as a pleasant surprise?

---

* LDO—limited duty officer, a former enlisted man whose duties are limited to the area of his enlisted rating specialty.

Admiral Osborn: I did not expect it. It was a very pleasant surprise. I'm not being humble; I just didn't think there was a chance, mainly because of the one fitness report. Also, while the flag board was in process, I was on crutches and very visible. Most people knew it was a fairly serious problem, and the word does get around. So I figured the combination of the two would do me in.

Paul Stillwell: You must have had something else to offer to overcome both of those.

You mentioned Admiral Dunn. Did you want to say something specific about him?

Admiral Osborn: Only that he was very good to work for during the relatively short period we were together.

Paul Stillwell: I have gotten to know him through his Naval Institute connections and doing his oral history, and I have a lot of admiration for him.

Admiral Osborn: I was only in that job for three or four months. They needed to get me into a "joint" job. I had never been in a joint command, and they had a rule that you couldn't go to fleet command as a flag officer until you were "joint qualified" by virtue of serving in a joint staff billet.

The best opportunity to do that was to send me to the National Military Command Center as a watch team leader. The first slot open was two or three months down the road. In the meantime they needed someone to fill in as OP-11 for three months. So I had two flag jobs in the first six months. There isn't much to say about the OP-11 job. That office was responsible for Navy training policy, and it was a worthless staff because naval training policy was put together by the Chief of Naval Education and Training at Pensacola. He paid absolutely no attention to OP-01 in training matters. Any time there was a CEB (CNO Executive Board) involving education or training, he came to Washington and sat on the CEB. I shouldn't say that OP-11 was worthless, but it wasn't worth the manpower that was invested in the staff. It was dual effort, and this part of the dual wasn't making much impact.

Paul Stillwell: Was Admiral Zech still OP-01 at that time?[*]

Admiral Osborn: Yes he was. He was a very kind gentleman, a very wise man. I felt like he was doing a good job. I had a lot of contact with him in both the distribution director job and the OP-11 job. In the personnel job I saw him practically daily. The only thing at issue with Admiral Zech, he was not a quick decision-maker. There was always a jam up to get something through him, a very slow process. His EA at that time was Tony Maness, who had been my administrative officer in VP-40.[†] Tony was a very able administrator. He had a tough time keeping things moving. It wasn't a streamlined process.

Paul Stillwell: You talked about the submariners being very well specialized and trained in their specialty. This was a non-technical job for a technical person.

Admiral Osborn: A capable man. He had been ComNavForJapan at one time. A lot of people thought that OP-01 was a pretty slow process. From there I went to the National Military Command Center (NMCC). I would say it was one of the most enjoyable and interesting jobs of my time in the Navy.

Paul Stillwell: What made it so?

Admiral Osborn: The structure at that time was five watch teams. We were on a shift schedule. We stood the same eight-hour shift for eight days and then had four days off. Upon return, we would be on the shift that was eight hours later on the clock, so, in the course of three cycles, we stood a set of watches for each of the eight-hour periods of the clock. There were five teams, each headed by a flag or general officer. We were the end of the funnel for all DoD information from around the world. All new happenings or incidents of note came to the command center. When something happened anywhere in

---

[*] Vice Admiral Lando W. Zech, Jr., USN, Chief of Naval Personnel.
[†] Captain Anthony R. Maness, USN.

the world, the information came to NMCC first. Team members were from all services, as well as DIA, CIA, NSA, and FBI. An OpRep came in there first, and it was our job to decide what to do with it and who to notify.[*]

Paul Stillwell: So it requires a considerable degree of judgment.

Admiral Osborn: A lot of judgment calls. As an example, my team was on when the Beirut bombing took place, and also, when KAL 007, Korean airliner, was shot down by the Soviets over Sakhalin.[†] We had the conn when Lieutenant Commander Schaufelberger was assassinated in El Salvador.[‡] You are a conduit and a decision-maker on how to deal with each incident. Whether to call the director of the Joint Staff, part of it is to recommend to him who else should be notified, up to and including the Chairman of the Joint Chiefs and the Secretary of Defense. You find yourself calling the SecDef at 3:00 A.M. and convincing him your information is important enough to wake him up.

Paul Stillwell: Are you saying that these people don't necessarily have the philosophy of the skipper who says, "If in doubt, call me"?

Admiral Osborn: Most of the time, no problem. Occasionally you would get an earful. It was exciting from that standpoint, handling that and dealing with all the key people. The most important purpose of the NMCC was the nuclear threat. We drilled continuously on procedures for the nuclear threat. We had a direct tie with NORAD.[§] We had a visual monitor which showed the threat at the same time NORAD saw it. They would issue a "threat warning" if they thought it was a real threat. It was our

---

[*] OpRep—operational report.
[†] On 23 October 1983, a suicide terrorist drove a truck filled with the equivalent of 12,000 pounds of explosives into the Marine Corps barracks in Beirut, Lebanon. The resulting explosion killed 241 Americans and wounded 70. On 1 September 1983 a Soviet SU-15 fighter aircraft shot down a Boeing 747 passenger plane over the Sea of Japan. The 269 people in the plane were all killed. The Korean Airlines plane was on flight 007, which was en route from Anchorage, Alaska, to Seoul, South Korea, but strayed off course and violated Soviet airspace over Sakhalin Island.
[‡] On the evening of 25 May 1983, Lieutenant Commander Albert Schaufelberger III, USN, deputy commander of the U.S. military assistance advisory group in El Salvador, was shot and killed by gunmen who fired into his car when it was parked outside the University of Central American in San Salvador.
[§] NORAD—North American Air Defense Command.

responsibility to deal with the warning and decide whether to proceed with it as a real threat. If so, a threat warning conference would bring in all the CinCs and the Chairman, JCS.

As the head of the watch team you would then make a recommendation on whether to proceed to the next level, which was to inform the SecDef, and he would then decide whether to bring in the President. The Soviets would launch test missiles constantly, so almost every watch there would be a missile coming out of the Soviet Union. Aside from that, we did regular drills where a multiple missile launch would be simulated, and all the communications procedures would be executed as if it were the real thing. Surrogates would act in place of the principals such as the President, SecDef, Chairman, etc. We would go through the several stages of threat warning and practice the whole process including course of action recommendations.

Paul Stillwell: If launches happen that often, how are you going to know if it is the real thing?

Admiral Osborn: That is the job of the NORAD system. Of course, launch of one missile is not likely to be a threat. On one occasion, back in the '80s, a computer glitch caused a false picture of multiple missiles. I don't know the details, but it got everyone's attention.

Paul Stillwell: You mentioned the Beirut bombing. Please discuss that event.

Admiral Osborn: It was in the middle of the night, so the principals had gone home. That was a case where it was clear from the initial information that the Chairman and SecDef plus a lot of others needed to know right away.* Before long we had flag and general officers in the command center by the bunch. Our job was to keep the information flowing to the decision-makers. In the aftermath, there was a lot of

---

* General John W. Vessey, Jr., USA, served as Chairman of the Joint Chiefs of Staff from 18 June 1982 to 30 September 1985. Caspar W. Weinberger served as Secretary of Defense from 21 January 1981 to 23 November 1987.

speculation and discussion about whether it could have been prevented. At the time, General Crist (later CentCom) was the assistant to Director, Joint Staff.* He was less than helpful. He went ballistic. It probably related to his being a Marine, which is understandable. That bombing occupied everyone's attention for a long time and gave the Chairman a lot of headaches.

Paul Stillwell: You mentioned also the downing of the Korean airliner.

Admiral Osborn: That was a strange one because the information was so scant. There was no way of knowing what really happened for a long time. As we began to get information from various observation points, it began to be suspect that the plane had been shot down over Soviet territory. The first question was why the airplane was over Soviet territory. There was all kinds of speculation, but it was three or four days before the facts came out. They had set their navigation system incorrectly in Anchorage before takeoff. Of course, we had information from several listening posts about communication between the Soviet pilots and their controller. My job was to notify people and keep them informed.

Paul Stillwell: What do you recall about Lieutenant Commander Schaufelberger?

Admiral Osborn: We had received word of a problem in El Salvador but didn't have any details. A call came through to me from a Mr. Schaufelberger.† He said he had just seen on CNN that his son was shot in El Salvador.‡ He said, "The Navy Command Center will not confirm my son has been killed; they won't tell me anything." I asked him to hold and called the Navy Command Center to see what they knew. The Navy Command Center said they could not release anything yet and needed more information. At that point we received official information from El Salvador, so I confirmed for the father that his son had been killed. That was not my job; it was the Navy's job. So I immediately

---

* Major General George B. Crist, USMC, Vice Director, Joint Staff.
† The father of the dead officer was Captain Albert A. Schaufelberger, Jr., USN (Ret.), a naval aviator.
‡ CNN—Cable News Network.

called back to the Navy Command Center and brought them up to date. Being a former Navy pilot, the father knew the structure well enough to know the NMCC was the next level up from the Navy Command Center. When I confirmed the son's death, Mr. Schaufelberger said that it was terrible news, but that he and his wife wanted to thank me for giving them the facts.

A couple of other things about the job that were a little different. At one point we went to the underground alternate command center in Maryland to conduct a worldwide exercise simulating a nuclear attack on Washington. General Stilwell played the role of President, and I played the Chairman JCS in the exercise.[*] General Stillwell was quite an interesting personage. He was a wise old owl, a classic. I got him to tell me the "cherry tree story" from his tour as commander of Army forces in Korea.[†] It was a fairly long exercise, about a week, I believe. We didn't see daylight for the entire time since we were underground. We lived pretty well—good quarters and food.

Paul Stillwell: I suspect that the place was pretty well stocked because of the potential that the nation's command structure would have to survive there for quite a little while.

Admiral Osborn: The NORAD information and warning system is hooked into that command center, just as it is at the NMCC in the Pentagon.

Also, on two occasions during that tour, my watch team launched in the NEACAP aircraft (nuclear emergency airborne command post) for nuclear attack drills. Both times I played the role of the President. The NEACAP would take off and land at a field near D.C. to pick up the President from his helicopter. Then it would take off and then remain airborne as the drill played out.

---

[*] General Richard G. Stilwell, USA (Ret.), was then the Deputy Under Secretary of Defense for Policy in a civilian job, after having previously completed his active Army service.

[†] On 18 August 1976 a group of about 30 North Korean soldiers, who were wielding axes and metal pikes, killed two U.S. Army officers and wounded four Army enlisted men and five South Korean soldiers. Those who suffered the attack were part of a working party at Panmunjom in the demilitarized zone between North and South Korea. They had been in the process of trimming trees at the truce site in order to facilitate surveillance activities. At the time General Stilwell was Commander of United Nations and United States Forces in Korea.

Paul Stillwell: This was your first joint tour after nearly 30 years of Navy-only experience. What changes or differences did you observe?

Admiral Osborn: I suppose you feel more of a bureaucracy in the joint environment. It is a train slowly moving down the track. You know, a large oil tanker takes a long time to change direction. I also observed a lot of close coordination and cooperation amongst staff members at all levels. Had some wonderful people to work with and observe. Bob Herres (later to be the first Vice Chairman) was the three-star communicator on the JCS staff.* A very impressive man. General Prillaman was the J-3.† He was an old country boy from West Virginia. He was still a backwoods West Virginian wearing three stars. His plan was to go right back there when he retired.

Paul Stillwell: Did you get insights as to the way people from the other services approach problems that might be different from the Navy's way?

Admiral Osborn: It is hard to generalize on that one.

Paul Stillwell: The stereotype is that Navy people are more operationally oriented, and the Army/Air Force people have a better background in staff work.

Admiral Osborn: That is certainly true, particularly Army. Army folks have a much better background in staff work than we do. I first observed that at Fort Leavenworth. Lieutenant colonels had three or four commands under their belt by then. They were very efficient in staff planning and that kind of thing. To me, Air Force officers always look too good to be true, uniforms too perfect, teeth brushed too well—a little too slick for my blood. I developed a great deal of respect for Army officers at Fort Leavenworth. First of all, these guys had been shot at for two tours at least. They were real patriots. The

---

* General Robert T. Herres, USAF, served as Vice Chairman of the Joint Chiefs of Staff from 6 February 1987 to 28 February 1990.
† Lieutenant General Richard L. Prillaman, USA, Joint Staff Director for Operations.

Army is a little more old-fashioned in most things. The Air Force is a little too modern, and the Navy is somewhere in the middle.

Paul Stillwell: To revert to a Navy topic—at that time there was a Navy Secretary who cut a very wide swath, John Lehman.[*] Do you have any observations on him?

Admiral Osborn: A lot. Who doesn't? I did not know him personally. He came in when I was in NMPC. He tore us up like nobody's business. He had all these guys that he and Ace Lyons wanted to put in specific spots, and he wanted it done now.[†] Some didn't fit the spots, and some didn't have the experience for the job. He bent a lot of rules on flight time. He was aggrandizing himself as an A-6 bombardier/navigator, which didn't set well with a lot of aviators. I'm sure he had good reason for his personnel moves. He ran roughshod in order to do it and showed no respect for the personnel system. In my view, he didn't show any respect for the office of the CNO. I don't care how powerful and important you are, that is not a very good way to do business.

He did a lot of good for the Navy. He could have done much better if he worked with the CNO and showed some respect for the CNO's office. He brought in an Assistant Secretary for Research and Development by the name of Mel Paisley, who was a known crook.[‡] He was a known crook before he was put in the office and ended up in jail for what he did in office. John Lehman's star in history would have been a little brighter if he had used better judgment in dealing with people in the Navy. What he did in terms of 600 ships was remarkable and wonderful, so what he did was good.

Paul Stillwell: When he dictated these various assignments, were they executed the way he wanted?

---

[*] John F. Lehman, Jr., served as Secretary of the Navy from 5 February 1981 to 10 April 1987.
[†] Rear Admiral James A. Lyons, Jr., USN.
[‡] On 18 October 1991, a federal judge sentenced Melvyn R. Paisley, who had served as Assistant Secretary of the Navy in the Reagan Administration, to four years in prison and fined him $50,000. Paisley admitted receiving more than $3.3 million in kickbacks from various corporations for steering Navy contracts their way during his time in office.

Admiral Osborn: Yes, there really wasn't any choice. We would ask his office to consider the factors involved, but it usually didn't make any difference.

Paul Stillwell: I talked to Admiral Lawrence, who was later Chief of Naval Personnel.* He had a great sense of frustration and unhappiness over his relationship with the Secretary.

Admiral Osborn: Of course, the CNO was put in a terrible position many times, and he was bypassed often, only to find out after the fact.

Paul Stillwell: What is your Mel Paisley story?

Admiral Osborn: When I was WingsPac at Moffett Field later, Paisley had an A-3 that he used as his personal airplane to travel around the country. They landed at Moffett Field, and we put him and his wife in a VIP guest apartment above the garage of our quarters. I had just returned from Hawaii and had a case of pineapples sitting in the breezeway outside our door. He came out of his apartment, saw the pineapples, and helped himself to three or four. I think that this was his mode of operation. He didn't think the rules were made for him, but he eventually got caught.

Paul Stillwell: One other thing we didn't talk about in connection with NMPC, that was the time when Secretary Lehman was pushing strongly to bring battleships back into commission.† What requirements did that impose on NMPC to man those ships.

Admiral Osborn: That was a tough one. We really had to do some scratching to fill the billets. They had to be good people. It was top priority and top quality, and was difficult. There was no question we were going to do it, and do it right, but that meant some extraordinary detailing actions. Pulling people out of jobs early, some real personal

---

* Vice Admiral William P. Lawrence, USN, served as Chief of Naval Personnel from 28 September 1983 to 31 December 1985.
† During the 1980s, all four of the Iowa (BB-64)-class battleships were reactivated from mothballs and rejoined the fleet.

hardships. It was a challenge. That same kind of thing happened when they decided to form SEAL Team Six.* I was given the job of covering the fact that we were even detailing to that organization. Their records were all covered, so there was no way you could ever tell where they were.

Paul Stillwell: What brought that about?

Admiral Osborn: That was the Navy component of Delta Force at Fort Bragg, only they were at Little Creek, Virginia.†

Paul Stillwell: I take it that has since become public knowledge.

Admiral Osborn: One of the officers, Richard Marcinko, has since written a number of books.‡ He got in a lot of trouble in that job because he lived fast and loose with the rules. He was pretty much an independent command with not much oversight.

Paul Stillwell: You then went to command Patrol Wings Pacific. This was the job at Moffett, and this is the pinnacle for a patrol plane aviator, isn't it?

Admiral Osborn: Absolutely. We had three previous tours at Moffett, so it was going back to a place we knew well, and it was where I wanted to go. It was a great job. The first thing I would mention is that I focused on safety. Only a few months before, a young Naval Academy graduate, football star, had flathatted at Pago Pago and flew his plane into the hotel, killing the crew and people in the hotel. In the course of the investigation of the accident, it came out that he had been breaking all kinds of flight

---

* SEALs are Navy personnel trained for sea, air, and land operations. In previous years similar individuals were designated as part of underwater demolition teams (UDTs). In addition to that specialty, the SEALs have a broader mission that includes commando-type operations ashore.
† Delta Force is a component of the Special Forces Command.
‡ Captain Richard Marcinko, USN (Ret.), has written a number of books. The first and probably best known is Rogue Warrior: the Explosive Autobiography of the Controversial Death-Defying Founder of the Navy's Top Secret Counterterrorist Unit—Seal Team Six (New York: Pocket Books, 1992).

rules for a long period of time. I began flying with crews as much as I could and doing a lot of looking around. It became clear that a little belt tightening was necessary.

I did a lot of writing on safety, put together two videos. One was a presentation I made to the entire squadron of VP-31, the readiness training squadron. I took all the major P-3 accidents and dissected each one as to cause. The video was required viewing by all squadrons in the fleet. The second round, I went to each squadron personally and gave a safety presentation to all hands.

It was a great time to have that job, because the Soviets were just operating all over the place in the Eastern Pacific. The command structure was such that I had operational control of all the maritime forces in the eastern Pacific. CTF 72 in Japan had control of Seventh Fleet forces. Any Soviet submarine that came toward the U.S. was our responsibility. We almost always had an SSBN that we were prosecuting. At one time, we were prosecuting six attack submarines at the same time, which was unprecedented.

Paul Stillwell: When you say prosecuting, what does that entail?

Admiral Osborn: First, going out and locating them and then staying with them, tracking them till they went home. We could usually do that successfully with the SSBNs, because we had the help of the SOSUS system. The attack submarines were quieter and operated close to the coast, so the SOSUS system wasn't always a help. The Victors, and Oscars later, were very quiet, so they were hard to pick up.*

Paul Stillwell: Did you tie in with surface ships on these occasions?

Admiral Osborn: Yes, we did. In the summer of '86 we had one big exercise in mid-Pacific in an area midway between Seattle and Hawaii in what we called the big hole area. It was known as the big hole because it was near the limit of operation for the P-3,

---

* Soviet Oscar I-class nuclear-powered, guided missile submarines began entering active service in the early 1980s. They displaced 11,500 tons on the surface and 14,500 tons submerged; length, 479 feet; beam, 59 feet; draft, 33 feet; speed 33 knots. They were armed with torpedoes and surface-to-surface missiles.

no matter where they were based. At one point, we had six ships with towed arrays and helicopters. We had a big force and were working three Soviet submarines at the same time.

Paul Stillwell: You had operational control. How much time did you have with Commander Third Fleet?

Admiral Osborn: A lot, because he was the overall commander. The surface force commander, Jonathan Howe, also reported to him.

Paul Stillwell: What more do you have to say about that big exercise?

Admiral Osborn: It was an interesting relationship with Jonathan Howe. He was in charge of the exercise units. He really didn't have a good feel for what the P-3 could do. He strongly suggested some things that just weren't going to work. We had some personal messages back and forth and got it pretty well sorted out. When it was all said and done, he wasn't totally convinced I was fully cooperative. His after-action report was a tad bit biased. He took most of the credit for the successes, which wasn't quite the case. Frankly, the ship crews learned more than we did, because they were doing something they didn't normally get a chance to do. Contact with Soviet submarines was very rare for them. We were doing what we normally did, except for the air/surface coordination, which was a good learning experience for our crews.

Paul Stillwell: Is this just because of the nature of the platforms that the patrol planes are more likely to be able to detect them?

Admiral Osborn: First of all, you must have cued intelligence to get you in the vicinity of the submarine. The surface ships were never in the business of pouncing on a contact from SOSUS. That wasn't their mission, so this special exercise gave them a rare opportunity of operating in the open ocean against a Soviet submarine.

Paul Stillwell: Would they be more likely to have that kind of an occurrence in the Med?

Admiral Osborn: Definitely, but their intelligence would not be from SOSUS in the Med. Med submarine contacts generated from a range of other kinds of intelligence.

Paul Stillwell: What were some of the things that you learned from that experience?

Admiral Osborn: The one that stands out is better communications. Good communications allow the coordinating commander to have a better understanding of what you are thinking and for you to gain a better understanding of what he is thinking. Getting everybody on the same sheet of music and approaching everything in the same way. Historically that is the first bugaboo of any coordinated operation. This is not completely an electronic problem. Some of it is taking more care in written communication to provide the proper information to the person on the other end of the line. In the case of this exercise, voice communication between Admiral Howe and myself was very difficult, due to system limitations. Satellite communication has improved tremendously since then.

Paul Stillwell: That is the reason you had so many drills, for example, when you were in the military command center.

Admiral Osborn: That's right. It was a rather synthetic environment, because you wouldn't normally send that many ships, that far, to a point in the middle of the ocean to prosecute a sub, or subs. There would be too great a risk the sub would be gone. In this case SOSUS and VP were holding an SSBN, so there was a degree of confidence that contact would still be held when the ships got there.

Paul Stillwell: Was there any concern that by responding in that fashion that the Soviets would be tipped off of the SOSUS capability.

Admiral Osborn: Yes, that was always a consideration with the use of SOSUS cuing. It was a risk you took every time, and the Soviets knew we could get good contact with them when they were in their missile launch "box," so it wasn't going to be any surprise to them when we got contact. We tried to be careful as much as we could.

Paul Stillwell: Did you see a measurable improvement in safety as a result of your emphasis on that point?

Admiral Osborn: It is hard to measure how safely your crews are operating. The only quantitative measurement you have is the NATOPS ground testing and flight evaluations all crews go through once a year. You get a fair feel there. What you don't get is a sense of cavalier kinds of activity like the pilot at Pago Pago was into, tendency to show off, laxness in the rules. Also, you don't sense complacency, which is the root of many accidents. So it's hard to measure. What you try to do is instill in the commanding officer a strong sense that safety has to be the number-one thing to think about. Even in wartime, safety has to be at the top, but there you take the urgency of the mission into account and temper your actions accordingly. Consideration of safety must be paramount in all operations. So if you instill it in commanding officers and feel comfortable they are on board, and have the message, that is what command is all about. You really have to leave it up to them, except for any observations you make, either informally, or through formal evaluations. I could fly with a crew and immediately tell whether they were putting on for me, or whether they weren't. I could tell by the way they were operating whether they were in the habit of doing things right.

Paul Stillwell: How could you tell by operating with the squadron whether they usually operated that way, or whether they were faking it?

Admiral Osborn: I had flown in the P-3 so much, and been at each crew position so much, that it was easy to tell by their actions whether they were functioning for my benefit, or whether it was standard procedure. You talk to the crew members and ask them questions. Enlisted crew members are very open. You find out all kinds of things, which they probably wish afterward that they hadn't said.

Paul Stillwell: What kinds of things?

Admiral Osborn: You are talking about how you operate and, for example, discussing procedures for takeoff and landing, you kind of lead into it. They might blurt out that they don't worry about this or that procedure in their crew. I was most interested in how the flight station (cockpit) team handled takeoffs and landings, as well as the other procedures throughout the flight.

Paul Stillwell: How much of the time did you spend flying?

Admiral Osborn: In the WingsPac job, not a whole lot. I would try to fly once a week. My wing commanders were on board with the safety philosophy, so they were flying and observing more frequently. They, in turn, sensitized their commanding officers to make safety a way of life.

Paul Stillwell: What memories do you have of the wing commanders who reported to you?

Admiral Osborn: They were all exceptionally good people. I relied on them a great deal and left things to them. I took a hands-off approach on specific things with them. I did continue to hammer the safety aspects and tried to ensure they fully understood the importance of it, that they spent a lot of time on it, and conveyed that essence to their commanding officers. I think that worked pretty well. They were all very capable.

Paul Stillwell: Management by exception?

Admiral Osborn: Yes, my main concerns were tactical operations, training policy, and budget issues. I had five air stations and eight ASWOCs (antisubmarine operations centers), the command centers for ASW operations. With 14 squadrons, the budget and training issues for that whole force took care of my time. Plus, there were speaking engagements and other administrative functions.

Paul Stillwell: How much VIP entertainment did you undertake?

Admiral Osborn: When I wasn't on travel, we entertained about three nights a week. That was without mess specialists, although they would moonlight for us, and I would pay them. We could not have done it without that.

Paul Stillwell: Who were the recipients of these speeches you made?

Admiral Osborn: Primarily changes of command, occasionally in town to various groups.

A couple of things on the negative side. Shortly after moving into that position, I had a visit from a young lieutenant who had recently detached from one of the squadrons. He was convincing enough to my secretary that they recommended I talk to him. The officer told me the commanding officer of his former squadron had carried on a visible affair with the squadron female intelligence officer while on deployment to Diego Garcia. He also accused the CO of showing favoritism to the female officer, including award recommendations she didn't rate. After talking with him I was pretty much convinced this was something that needed to be investigated.

I contacted Admiral Dan Wolkensdorfer, whom I had relieved, and asked him if he knew of anything that was going on in this regard.[*] He admitted to me he was aware that there was a problem and had decided not to do anything about it. I couldn't leave it at that, because the accusations were a blatant disregard for naval regulations, clear fraternization, and misuse of command position. I convened an Article 32 investigation, which led to a general court-martial, where he was convicted.[†] It was very distasteful, particularly distasteful to me because I had to clean up someone else's dirty laundry.

---

[*] Rear Admiral Daniel J. Wolkensdorfer, USN.
[†] This is a reference to a procedure prescribed in Article 32 of the Uniform Code of Military Justice.

Paul Stillwell: It was distasteful enough on the face of it. What was the outcome? Was he dismissed?

Admiral Osborn: No, he wasn't dismissed, but he was confined to quarters and lost part of his retirement. He didn't get a real heavy hit, possibly because he was about to retire anyway.

Paul Stillwell: Was the Naval Investigative Service involved in it, and did the intelligence officer also face disciplinary action?

Admiral Osborn: Yes, the NIS was involved. She was not disciplined, because there really wasn't anything I felt like we could make stick. I would have liked to, because she had a very bad attitude about the whole thing. She was very smug and did not have a good reputation amongst her peers.

Paul Stillwell: Was the skipper married while this was going on?

Admiral Osborn: Yes, he was, as a matter of fact. His wife was aware beforehand.
    The other negative item was a complaint against my flag secretary that he had sexually abused a juvenile female in his office. I had it investigated and ordered him to mast. I dismissed it because, in my view, the weight of evidence was not there. About a year later he was caught doing the same thing with someone else at another command.

Paul Stillwell: Which was even a worse offense than the one you described earlier, because, at least, you had consulting adults in the first one.

Admiral Osborn: I suspected that there was something there, but there just wasn't enough to convict him. At least I didn't feel there was.

Paul Stillwell: This was a period when women were coming more and more into naval aviation. Did you have woman pilots and NFOs in your squadrons.

Admiral Osborn: No, we only had enlisted at that time.

I had two bosses in that job. ComNavAirPac was my administrative senior, and Com3rdFlt was my operational senior. AirPac was Jim Service and Pete Easterling.[*] Third Fleet was Duke Hernandez and Ken Moranville.[†]

Paul Stilwell: Anything to bring out on any of those gentlemen?

Admiral Osborn: No, except I was disappointed to find out that Ken Moranville got himself across the breakers later.[‡]

Paul Stillwell: When he was Com6thFlt.

Admiral Osborn: Those things are always very troubling. They shouldn't happen. You have to wonder about someone who is smart enough to advance as an officer in the Navy and then be so stupid to do that kind of thing, number one, and to think they were going to get away with it, number two.

Paul Stillwell: I suspect it was part of the culture, and it had been done for years. Then the rules changed, and people became more accountable.

---

[*] Vice Admiral Crawford A. Easterling, USN, served as Commander Naval Air Force Pacific Fleet from 4 August 1982 to 16 August 1985. Vice Admiral James E. Service, USN, served in the billet from 16 August 1985 to 21 August 1987.

[†] The following officers served in succession as Commander Third Fleet: Vice Admiral Kendall E. Moranville, USN, from September 1985 to June 1986; Vice Admiral Huntington Hardisty, USN, from June 1986 to August 1986; Vice Admiral Diego E. Hernandez, USN, from August 1986 to January 1989.

[‡] On 20 August 1988 Vice Admiral Kendall E. Moranville, USN, was relieved as Commander Sixth Fleet. He had been under consideration for another three-star job until 19 August, when he received a letter of reprimand as the result of an admiral's mast. He was charged with improprieties involving travel claims and in becoming accompanied by an unauthorized female Italian civilian while flying U.S. military aircraft when he was Commander Sixth Fleet. The Chief of Naval Operations, Admiral Carlisle A. H. Trost, USN, forced Moranville to retire as a rear admiral, one level below his highest active duty rank.

Admiral Osborn: That was probably the case with him, although he was well aware that the rules had changed. Another flag officer I knew well was in command when he was brought to task for misuse of a Navy airplane and other things outside of Navy Regulations. He should have known better and did know better.

One final item on that job. Not long after arriving, it was time to select a new personal aide. We put the word out in the squadrons, and there were four eager candidates. Three of the interviewees were straightforward, and I was impressed with them all. The fourth was an officer by the name of Walter Kreitler.* He was a very gregarious gentleman, and he went overboard to try to impress me with his qualifications and desire for the position. I was actually slightly taken aback by his demeanor. He just didn't fit my personality. However, the more I thought about him, the more I was convinced to take a chance. He turned out to be one of the joys of that tour and remains a close family friend. We look on him as an added son. He has since been very successful in the Navy and should be a flag officer one day. He is an extraordinary leader of men and women.

Paul Stillwell: You then went to Defense Mapping Agency as deputy director. How did that assignment come about?

Admiral Osborn: I suppose the Peter Principle took effect, and the Navy decided it was time for me to do other things for a living.† I received orders to the Defense Mapping Agency (DMA), which was quite a nice experience, and very interesting from the standpoint of personalities. The director was a gentleman by the name of Bob Rosenberg, who was an Air Force two-star.‡ A very fiery, competent officer who knew Washington well. He had served on the National Security Council under Brzezinski.§

---

* Lieutenant Walter M. Kreitler, USN, a naval flight officer, now a captain.
† The concept was first introduced by Laurence J. Peter and Raymond Hull in a humorous book, The Peter Principle (New York: Morrow, 1969) that described the pitfalls of bureaucratic organization. The original principle stated that in a hierarchically structured organization, people tend to be promoted up to their "level of incompetence." In other words, they keep being promoted until they reach a job they can't do well.
‡ Major General Robert A. Rosenberg, USAF.
§ Zbigniew K. Brzezinski served as President Jimmy Carter's National Security Adviser from 1977 to 1981.

He came into the agency when it was very bloated, had not had a housecleaning in a long time. The agency had about 9,000 people, including 33 Senior Executive Service (SES)-level executives. Rosenberg had arrived just a few months before me and had begun to set about cleaning house from the top down. After I had worked for him a few weeks, he made me his hatchet man and gave me the job of doing some of the dirty work. Some of the SES executives needed to go. They had been there too long, the classic DoD civilians who had passed their prime. This came at a time when the agency was in a tremendous revolutionary state. Map making had always been a paper process under the pens of cartographers. We were introducing a totally new digital process with much of the base data coming from satellite imagery. The installation of the equipment and training of the personnel was all in process, millions and millions of dollars worth of equipment.

Paul Stillwell: And a lot of the people who had been there a long time probably did not have that background.

Admiral Osborn: Most didn't have the background, and some were not prepared to learn. This was quite a change, pretty sophisticated stuff. Technical skills that were totally foreign to these people. I was there a little over a year, and it was a great experience. There was never a dull moment when working for Bob Rosenberg. He was a dynamo and was making big changes. There was a lot of hate and discontent flying around the halls, and he gave me the job of doing the job performance evaluations on these senior executives. It was interesting. He certainly made some progress, and I think I made a contribution to the organization. I learned a little about mapping and took advantage of that to a degree by later working for two different mapping companies for short periods of time. It was a positive experience. It was a good way to go out.

Paul Stillwell: You say it was bloated. Did you get rid of billets as well as people?

Admiral Osborn: Yes, it is very hard in the civil service to fire an individual, so the cleaning out and downsizing was mostly by attrition.

Paul Stillwell: Was there some humane factor to take care of these people and help them find other jobs to ease the transition?

Admiral Osborn: At the lower levels attrition was mostly from billets that were deleted due to the change from manual cartography to digital map production. At the higher levels, some people were retirement age and realized they didn't have a future in the new system, so they retired. You can juggle things around so it is pretty painless.

Paul Stillwell: Did you have any people whose billets were eliminated involuntarily, from their standpoint?

Admiral Osborn: We had a few of those. We almost invariably found them another job in DoD. The senior people who were really producers got on board with the new system, learned the process, and were put in responsible positions. We had heart-to-heart talks with a few of the SES-level executives and they saw it was time to retire gracefully. We had several facilities: St. Louis, San Antonio, Louisville, and several in the D.C. area. At that time our headquarters was on the grounds of the Naval Observatory. A short time later the headquarters moved to a new building in Merryfield.

Paul Stillwell: What advantage is gained from using these new technologies?

Admiral Osborn: Greater accuracy and greater ease in upgrading maps. One of the most difficult things is keeping maps updated with respect to borders, country names, city names, etc. One of the biggest advantages was that overhead (satellite) imagery showed contour information with accuracy. In the Soviet Union we had sparse information in many areas and incorrect contour information in others. All that could be cleaned up with imagery input. This was the case in many parts of the world.

Paul Stillwell: Did you have to equip ships and other stations with equipment that could receive this updated map or chart?

Admiral Osborn: No, not really. Every unit or ship is on distribution for a certain set of maps or charts. When an update is published, it is automatically mailed to them.

Paul Stillwell: You were still doing paper printing.

Admiral Osborn: When I say we were building digital maps, they were paper maps produced from digital imagery, using digital production processes. Now there are a lot of digital maps going out. We were also producing all the information for Tomahawk missile guidance.[*] By using imagery as a source for the mapping information we were able to give them a much better guidance product. At that time, the Tomahawk guided itself by comparing the built-in track data with what it actually saw on the ground, and that is how it changed course and guided to the target. The more accurate the picture built into the missile, the more accurate the flight path.

Paul Stillwell: My impression, rightly or wrongly, is that the Tomahawk now uses a satellite-based system.

Admiral Osborn: I believe you are right, but that was after my involvement.

Paul Stillwell: Did the DMA have a role in the late 1980s in developing GPS?[†]

Admiral Osborn: No, not directly.

Paul Stillwell: I believe the name of the agency has changed and is now the National Imagery and Mapping Agency. Does that mean a move away from Defense Department emphasis?

---

[*] Tomahawk is a long-range cruise missile that entered the fleet in the early 1980s, capable of delivering either conventional or nuclear warheads. Originally conceived to have both antiship and land-attack versions, the antiship type is no longer in service. For details see Miles A. Libbey III, "Tomahawk," U.S. Naval Institute Proceedings, May 1984, pages 150-163.

[†] GPS—Global Positioning System, a satellite-based navigation system that provides terminals on earth with their geographic positions.

Admiral Osborn: I don't know what is involved in that. I haven't had information about what changes were made in the mission and structure of the agency.

Paul Stillwell: What else do you recall about that tour of duty?

Admiral Osborn: I met and worked with a tremendous number of really professional civilians—just as dedicated as you or I. They had a real sense of pride in their work. They knew that the fighting forces couldn't do anything without maps.

Paul Stillwell: You said facetiously that the Navy was preparing you for a career change. Were there any opportunities for active duty billets after that?

Admiral Osborn: No, that was my last. I had missed promotion twice. That was the determining factor.

Paul Stillwell: What kind of reaction, both mental and emotional, did you have in taking the uniform off after all those years?

Admiral Osborn: You should ask my wife that question. She would give you a more candid answer than I probably will.

Paul Stillwell: Why don't you give me your answer and then give me what you think she would say.

Admiral Osborn: In retrospect I didn't transition very well. The first time I missed promotion, I really thought I was competitive. There wasn't much chance the second time around, so it was kind of inevitable. The Navy had become so much a part of me that it was really hard to leave. Once I left, it was a hard transition to being a civilian and getting on with doing something meaningful, and getting over it. It took a lot of time, actually a couple of years to really become totally productive again, which was kind of a waste of time.

Paul Stillwell: How did you spend those two years?

Admiral Osborn: I worked for the state of Maine for a short time. It was a nothing job. The mistake we made was deciding to move to Maine, where we wanted to live. What I should have done was take a good job at whatever location it existed. We would have been better off. We loved Maine and still do, but we should have taken geographic location as the chips fell, job wise. I give people that advice when they want to talk about it. Go to the job and take the location. Don't go to a location and look for a job. That applies at any time for everyone.

Getting back to your question, I next worked for DeLorme Mapping Company. They are one of the leaders in travel maps, both paper and digital. They have a nice system now that uses GPS to track you accurately in your car and show you the way to any point. At the time I was there, they had a number of defense contracts with agencies like CIA, DIA and NSA. I managed those programs for about two years and then had a hip operation. We then went to Australia for about 18 months with Martin Marietta. That turned out to be a very good experience in every respect. I also spent a year in D.C. helping put together a nonprofit foundation, which was stimulating. It didn't pay a cent but was good nonetheless.

Paul Stillwell: You were teaching yourself that there can be life after the Navy.

Admiral Osborn: Just a little slow, that's all. Cathy would say about the same thing I did but a little more strongly.

Paul Stillwell: That placed a burden on her, undoubtedly.

Admiral Osborn: Oh, it did, and she carried me through, as she always has.

Paul Stillwell: Maybe you could talk a little more about that and the role she played.

Admiral Osborn: She was the classic Navy wife in terms of being supportive and being willing to put up with the separations. She really raised our family, because I had nine or ten deployments of six months or more. That was during the time when our children were in the formative stage of grade school and after.

Paul Stillwell: And that is the sacrifice that our nation calls on people to make time and again.

Admiral Osborn: She was wonderful. She kept her cool, most of the time, and did what she had to do. There was never a question in her mind about me staying in the Navy.

Paul Stillwell: That can be a major factor to get people out if they don't have that support.

Admiral Osborn: If they don't have it, they probably should not stay in. That is a general statement, but it is pretty close to true. If they don't have it, they are going to have marital problems.

Paul Stillwell: What did you do after Australia?

Admiral Osborn: I consulted for another mapping company for about a year, followed by another hip operation. Since that time I haven't worked for pay.

Paul Stillwell: What is your life routine now?

Admiral Osborn: Pretty relaxed. Play a little golf. Actually I work at a golf course one day a week and have golf privileges. We recently sold the large home we were in, purchased and rebuilt a smaller house, and did a major downsizing of possessions. That took some work. Due to a medical condition my wife has, we cannot be in cold weather, so we have a place in Florida for the winters. We are in a good position now. I'll probably get a little lazy, but we are enjoying life.

Paul Stillwell: Please bring me up to date on your children.

Admiral Osborn: Our oldest, Bradley, is 42. He married two years ago, and they have a son who is a little over one year old. He is a sales executive with a chemical company that sells to paper mills. Brian is a lieutenant commander in the Navy and is currently working on his doctorate in computer science at the Naval Postgraduate School. They have three children. Tom is a lieutenant commander in the Navy and serving as the flag secretary to the superintendent of the Naval Academy. They have four children. Sarah Jane is a high school Latin teacher in Blacksburg, Virginia, and they have two children.

Paul Stillwell: It must be a source of great pride that two of your sons are carrying on the Navy tradition.

Admiral Osborn: It is, and they seem to be doing well. We are equally proud of our whole family. They have all done very well.

Paul Stillwell: We have talked about a lot of topics in this interview and one a few months ago. Do you have any summing up thoughts by way of benediction?

Admiral Osborn: Every place I left, I felt like I had earned the respect of the troops. To me that was one of the most important measures. I also left every outfit having made it a little bit better.

Paul Stillwell: If those are the two things, then you were a complete success. From what I heard from you, you derived a great deal of enjoyment along the way.

Admiral Osborn: I wouldn't trade it for anything.

Paul Stillwell: I am certainly grateful to you for making an additional contribution in the form of this oral history, because you have talked about things that no one else has. There are very few patrol plane pilots in the collection, you and Admiral Coughlin being among the few. I am grateful for that and look forward to adding this to the collection for scholars a long way into the future.

Index to the Oral History of
Rear Admiral Oakley E. Osborn,
U.S. Navy (Retired)

Adak, Alaska
   In the late 1950s Patrol Squadron 17 operated from this base in the Aleutians, 26-28, 33, 35, 69; in the mid-1980s some Japanese P-3s flew from Japan to California via Adak, 49; in the late 1960s Patrol Squadron 19 was based here for Pacific surveillance patrols, 66-68, 70-73; current conditions, 70

Aircraft Carriers
   Vulnerability of carriers to submarines because of withering of ASW assets, 91
   See also: names of individual carriers

Air Force, U.S.
   In the late 1950s a detachment of the Navy's Patrol Squadron 17 was based at Chitose Air Force Base, Japan, during a deployment to the Western Pacific, 23-24; in the 1950s the Chitose base was returned to the Japanese, 25; in the late 1950s Navy Patrol Squadron 17 flew ice reconnaissance flights out of Eielson Air Force Base in Alaska, 33-34

Air Warfare
   In the 1950s Soviet fighter aircraft attacked some American patrol planes, 32, 34

Alaska
   Varying weather coming from Siberia makes for difficult flying conditions in Alaska, 26-28, 69-71; in the late 1950s Patrol Squadron 17 operated from Adak, 26-28, 33, 35, 69; ice reconnaissance flights from Fairbanks, 33-34; in the late 1960s Patrol Squadron 19 was based at Adak for Pacific surveillance patrols, 66-68, 70-73; current conditions at Adak, 70

Aleutian Islands
   In the late 1950s Patrol Squadron 17 operated from a base at Adak in the Aleutians, 26-28, 33, 35, 69; in the late 1960s Patrol Squadron 19 was based at Adak for Pacific surveillance patrols, 66-68, 70-73; current conditions at Adak, 70

Anderson, Admiral George W., Jr., USN (USNA, 1927)
   As Chief of Naval Operations in the early 1960s, visited the new aircraft carrier Kitty Hawk (CVA-63) at North Island Naval Air Station, 53-54

Antisubmarine Warfare
   In the late 1950s and early 1960s the P2V Neptune had limited capability for antisubmarine work, 29-30; in the mid-1960s, Anti-Submarine Warfare Group Five, built around the aircraft carrier Bennington (CVS-20), deployed from Long Beach to the Western Pacific, 40-46; the specialized antisubmarine carriers were not

particularly effective in that role, 44; in the mid-1980s U.S., Australian, and Japanese aircraft took part in international ASW exercises, 49; in the mid-1960s patrol planes operated near Yankee Station off Vietnam when CVS carriers were not available, 55-56; use of SOSUS in the 1960s and 1980s for the tracking of Soviet submarines in the Pacific, 59, 67-68, 138-141; a U.S. ASW exercise in the mid-1980s involved a variety of assets, 68, 138-139; in the mid-1970s OP-594 dealt with antisubmarine warfare readiness and training, 83-86; vulnerability of aircraft carriers to submarines because of withering of ASW assets, 91; in the late 1970s the various communities involved in ASW work had their own separate budget issues and needs, 97-98; development of dedicated ships to operated towed sonar arrays, 98; as commander of Patrol Wings Pacific Fleet in 1971-72, Rear Admiral Edward Waller developed a structured program for ASW crew training, 106; successful operations against Soviet submarines in the late 1970s, 112-113

Anti-Submarine Warfare Group Five
In the mid-1960s, while based on board the carrier <u>Bennington</u> (CVS-20), deployed to the Western Pacific, 40-46, 104; not particularly effective in the ASW role, 44; in October 1965 ran into a typhoon while en route from the Western Pacific to California, 49-50

Army Air Forces, U.S.
During World War II flew difficult fighter missions from the Aleutians, 69

Army Command and General Staff College, Fort Leavenworth, Kansas
In the early 1970s provided staff training for officers from various services and foreign countries, 73-75; Osborn's favorable observations on the Army officers in the school, 134-135

Atlantic Fleet, U.S.
When he was Commander in Chief Atlantic Fleet in the mid-1970s, Admiral Isaac Kidd did not put up with infringement from OpNav on his operational prerogatives, 101; because of geographical proximity has greater access to the Pentagon than does the Pacific Fleet, 102-103

Atsugi Naval Air Station, Japan
In the spring of 1963 P-3 aircraft of Patrol Squadron 31 made a long-distance flight from Moffett Field in California to Atsugi, 37-38

Australia
In the mid-1980s U.S., Australian, and Japanese aircraft took part in international ASW exercises, 49

Aviation Officer Candidate School, Pensacola, Florida
In 1955 Osborn entered the pre-flight program, then took flight training itself, 9-15; in the mid-1980s son Brian Osborn went through the program, 13; students in this program do not get the well-rounded knowledge Naval Academy graduates do, 20

Barker, Commander Franklin H., USN
In the late 1960s, as commanding officer of Patrol Squadron 19, provided effective leadership, 65-66

Base Realignment and Closure
In the 1990s there was some progress in closing down unnecessary facilities but not enough, in Osborn's view, 89-90

Beirut, Lebanon
Reaction to the terrorist bombing in October 1983 of the Marine barracks in Beirut, 130-132

Bennington, USS (CVS-20)
In the mid-1960s served as flagship for Commander Anti-Submarine Warfare Group Five, which deployed to the Western Pacific, 40-46; in October 1965 ran into a typhoon while en route from the Western Pacific to California, 49-50

Boorda, Admiral Jeremy M., USN
As Chief of Naval Operations in the 1980s revised the fitness report format, not necessarily for the better, 22, 126

Brunswick, Maine, Naval Air Station
Winter weather sometimes makes it a difficult place from which to operate aircraft, 112

Budgetary Issues
Roles of Congress and the Department of Defense in developing budgets in the mid-1970s, 89-90

Caldwell, Rear Admiral Turner F., USN (USNA, 1935)
In the mid-1960s served as Commander Antisubmarine Warfare Group Five, 40-41; fondness for hunting, 41, 46

Carper, Lieutenant Thomas R., USN
In the early 1970s did an exceptional job as tactical coordinator in Patrol Squadron 40, later served as governor of Delaware and as a U.S. Senator, 77

Chitose Air Force Base, Japan
In the late 1950s a detachment of Patrol Squadron 17 was based here for a time during a deployment to the Western Pacific, 23-24; in the late 1950s the base was returned to the Japanese, 25

Clampet, Lieutenant James V., USN
In the late 1950s, as member of Patrol Squadron 17, was a patrol plane commander who flew the P2V Neptune, 23

Computers
   Development of computer programs in the mid-1970s for self-paced training of individuals, 93-94

Congress, U.S.
   Roles of Congress and the Department of Defense in developing budgets in the mid-1970s, 89-90; involvement in the early 1980s in Navy personnel assignments, 123-124

Conrad, Rear Admiral Peter C., USN (USNA, 1953)
   In the early 1980s gave strong backing to Osborn while head of personnel distribution in the Naval Military Personnel Command, 116

Coughlin, Lieutenant John T., USN (USNA, 1950)
   In the late 1950s, as a member of Patrol Squadron 17, commanded a detachment of planes at Adak, Alaska, when the squadron deployed, 28-29

Courts-Martial
   In the mid-1980s the commanding officer of a Pacific Fleet patrol squadron was court-martialed because of a sexual misconduct with a female intelligence officer in the squadron, 143-144

Cubi Point Naval Air Station, Subic Bay, Philippines
   In the Cubi Point officers' club in the mid-1960s naval aviators on liberty were involved in inappropriate behavior, 46

Daniel Boone, USS (SSBN-629)
   In the mid-1960s Rear Admiral Gene Fluckey and Rear Admiral Robert Macpherson spent an enjoyable time exchanging sea stories on board this submarine, 104

Defense Department
   Roles of Congress and the Department of Defense in developing budgets in the mid-1970s, 89-90

Defense Mapping Agency
   Reduction of bloated structure in the late 1980s, 146-148; in the 1980s the technology moved to the creation of maps in a digital process from satellite imagery, 147-149

Dental Corps, U.S. Navy
   In Osborn's view, this community is deficient in leadership skills, 114-115

Drugs-Illegal
   Impact in the early 1980s of the Navy's zero-tolerance drug policy, 119

El Salvador
In May 1983, while on duty as deputy commander of the U.S. military assistance advisory group in El Salvador, Lieutenant Commander Albert A. Schaufelberger III was shot and killed, 130, 132-133

Families of Servicemen
On a couple of occasions in the 1960s Osborn contemplated leaving the Navy because of the difficulties caused by separation from his family, 34-35, 51; issues in the early 1970s for families of members of Patrol Squadron 40, 80; challenges of assigning officers in the early 1980s when family issues were involved, 116-117

Fitness Reports
In the late 1950s it was not required, or typical, for commanding officers to show junior officers their fitness reports or to counsel them, 21, 24-25; in more recent years junior officers have paid too much attention to fitness reports, 21; in the 1980s and 1990s there was restructuring of the fitness report format in an attempt to counter grade inflation, 21-22, 126-127; in the late 1950s Osborn got a nearly unsatisfactory report after the unauthorized firing of aircraft flares, 24-25

Flight Training
Conducted in the mid-1950s at Pensacola, Florida, 16-18; multi-engine training in the mid-1950s at Hutchinson, Kansas, 19-20

Fluckey, Rear Admiral Eugene B., USN (USNA, 1935)
In the mid-1960s, while serving as ComSubPac, had an enjoyable time visiting with Rear Admiral Robert Macpherson on board the submarine Daniel Boone (SSBN-629) and exchanging sea stories, 104

Galbraith, Fran
Civil servant who had a great deal of expertise within the Bureau of Naval Personnel on flag officer matters, 122

Harpoon Missile
In July 1979 VP-23 was the first squadron to fire an operational Harpoon missile from a P-3 aircraft, 107-108

Hedges, Rear Admiral Ralph R., USN (USNA, 1952)
In the late 1970s, as Commander Patrol Wings Atlantic Fleet, did not go along with Osborn's proposal to fire a deficient squadron commanding officer, 109-110, 127

Hiroshima, Japan
In the late 1950s personnel from U.S. Navy Patrol Squadron 17 went sightseeing in Hiroshima and found the local people cool toward them, 34

Houser, Vice Admiral William D., USN (USNA, 1942)
Impressive officer who served in the mid-1970s as OP-05, Deputy Chief of Naval Operations (Air Warfare), 89

Howe, Rear Admiral Jonathan T., USN (USNA, 1957)
In the mid-1980s commanded a large surface action group during a naval exercise in the Pacific, 68, 139-140

Hudson, Lieutenant Colonel John S., USMC
In the mid-1950s served as a flight instructor at Pensacola Naval Air Station, 17

Hutchinson, Kansas, Naval Air Station
Site of multi-engine operational flight training in the mid-1950s at, 19-20

Intelligence
In the late 1950s Patrol Squadron 17 conducted reconnaissance flights looking for Soviet ships, 29, 31-34

Isaman, Rear Admiral Roy M., USN
In the mid-1960s served as Commander Patrol Force Seventh Fleet during support of Vietnam operations, 52-53, 59

Iowa (BB-61)-Class Battleships
Difficulties in the early 1980s in providing crews for the reactivated ships of the class as they returned to the fleet from mothballs, 136-137

Iwakuni, Japan
In the late 1950s Patrol Squadron 17 was based at Iwakuni during Western Pacific deployments, 23-24

Iwo Jima, Bonin Islands
In 1945 was invaded by U.S. Marines, 3-4; in 1994 Osborn visited the island, 4

Japan
In the late 1950s Patrol Squadron 17 was based at Iwakuni during Western Pacific deployments, 23-24; a detachment from the squadron operated for a time from Chitose Air Force Base on Hokkaido, 23-24; in the late 1950s squadron personnel went sightseeing in Hiroshima, 34; in 1963 a group of P-3 Orions made a long-distance flight from Moffett Field in California to Atsugi Naval Air Station in Japan, 37-38; in the mid-1960s Osborn was supposed to set up a visit for Rear Admiral Robert Macpherson with a Japanese admiral near Yokosuka, but the driver took Macpherson to the wrong place, 48-49; in the mid-1980s the U.S. Navy participated in international exercises with Japanese forces, 49

Kidd, Admiral Isaac C., Jr., USN (USNA, 1942)
When he was Commander in Chief Atlantic Fleet in the mid-1970s, did not put up with infringement from OpNav on his operational prerogatives, 101

Kitty Hawk, USS (CVA-63)
New aircraft carrier that the CNO, Admiral George Anderson, visited at North Island in the early 1960s, 53-54

Koch, Rear Admiral Ferdinand B., USN (USNA, 1946)
In the mid-1970s served as OP-59, director of the Air Warfare Division of OpNav, 88

Korea
In September 1983 a Soviet fighter plane short down a Korean airliner with 269 people on board, 131, 133

Kreitler, Lieutenant Walter M., USN
A gregarious individual, did a fine job in the mid-1980s as Osborn's aide and flag lieutenant, 146

Larson, Commander Richard, USN
In 1959-60, as commanding officer of Patrol Squadron 17, was a good leader but a screamer, 26

Lawrence, Vice Admiral William P., USN (USNA, 1951)
In the early 1980s, as superintendent of the Naval Academy, took care of getting his own commandant of midshipmen, 121-122

Leave and Liberty
In the late 1950s personnel from Patrol Squadron 17 went sightseeing in Hiroshima, Japan, 34; in the mid-1960s a group of officers from the air group of the aircraft carrier Bennington (CVS-20) wreaked havoc in a club at White Beach, Okinawa, 45; in the Cubi Point officers' club in the mid-1960s naval aviators on liberty in the Philippines were involved in inappropriate behavior, 46

Lebanon
Reaction to the terrorist bombing in October 1983 of the Marine barracks in Beirut, 130-132

Lehman, John F., Jr.
Efforts to control personnel assignments while serving in the early 1980s as Secretary of the Navy, 135-136

Long, Vice Admiral Robert L. J., USN (USNA, 1944)
In the mid-1970s was highly respected while serving as DCNO (Submarine Warfare), 99

Macpherson, Rear Admiral Robert A., USN (USNA, 1933)
In 1964-65 served as Commander Anti-Submarine Warfare Group Five, based on board the aircraft carrier Bennington (CVS-20), 42, 45-46, 48-49, 104; had an enjoyable time visiting with Rear Admiral Gene Fluckey on board the submarine Daniel Boone (SSBN-629) and exchanging sea stories, 104

Mapping
In the 1980s the technology within the Defense Mapping Agency moved to the creation of maps in a digital process from satellite imagery, 147-149

Marine Corps, U.S.
Osborn's brother Clif fought in World War II as a Marine rifleman, 3-4; 1945 invasion of Iwo Jima, 3-4; role of Marine drill instructors in the mid-1950s at Aviation Officer Candidate School in Pensacola, 10-13, 15; in the mid-1950s Marine aviators served as flight instructors at Pensacola Naval Air Station, 17-18; reaction to the terrorist bombing in October 1983 of the Marine barracks in Beirut, Lebanon, 130-132

Market Time, Operation
In the mid-1960s Commander Patrol Force Seventh Fleet ran patrol plane support of Operation Market Time off the coast of Vietnam, 52-55

Martin, Captain Edward H., USN (USNA, 1954)
Former Vietnam POW who served in the mid-1970s as executive assistant to the DCNO (Air Warfare), 93

McCain, Captain John S. III, USN (Ret.) (USNA, 1958)
During the Vietnam War was captured by the North Vietnamese, later wrote about his experiences in a book, 64-65

McDonnell Douglas Corporation
In the mid-1970s introduced a flight simulator with a computer-generated visual system, 84-85

Medical Corps, U.S. Navy
In Osborn's view, this community is deficient in leadership skills, 114-115, 128

Medical Problems
In the early 1980s Osborn had hip surgery as the result of arthritis and then had difficulty in being able to do his job, 124-125

Merryman, Captain Charles A., Jr., USN
In the early 1960s, while on the staff of ComNavAirPac, helped supervise the fleet introduction of the P-3 Orion, 36-37

Mine Warfare
In the late 1950s Patrol Squadron 17 did some mine-laying training with P2V Neptunes, 31; in the mid-1960s the staff of Patrol Force Seventh Fleet made plans for possible mining of North Vietnam, 57-58

Missiles
In July 1979 VP-23 was the first squadron to fire an operational Harpoon missile from a P-3 aircraft, 107-108; in the 1980s the Defense Mapping Agency was involved in terrain mapping to provide guidance for Tomahawk missiles, 149

Moffett Field Naval Air Station, Sunnyvale, California
In the early 1960s was the base for Patrol Squadron 31 as it trained aircrews for the new P-3 Orion, 36-39; in the mid-1980s some Japanese P-3s flew from Japan to Moffett Field via Adak, Alaska, 49

Moranville, Vice Admiral Kendall E., USN
In 1986 received a letter of reprimand for improprieties while he was serving as Commander Sixth Fleet, 145-146

National Military Command Center
Role of watch standers in the early 1980s in handling Defense Department issues, 129-133; early 1980s command post exercise in Maryland to simulate the reaction to a nuclear attack, 133

NATOPS (Naval Air Training and Operations Procedures System)
Role of in promoting aviation safety, 87-88, 141; in the late 1970s one of the squadrons within Patrol Wing Five failed its NATOPS inspection, 104-105

Naval Academy, Annapolis, Maryland
In the early 1980s, Vice Admiral William Lawrence, the superintendent of the academy, took care of getting his own commandant of midshipmen, 121-122

Naval Air Force Pacific Fleet
In the early 1960s oversaw the phase-in of the P-3 Orion into the Pacific Fleet, 36-37; parochialism on the staff between TacAir and patrol plane people, 39-40

Naval Aviation
Ongoing parochialism on between individuals in the Navy's TacAir and patrol plane communities, 39-40, 90-92; roles of Congress and the Department of Defense in developing budgets in the mid-1970s, 89-90

Naval Military Personnel Command
Role in the early 1980s in placing naval officers in a variety of billets in the staff corps and the various restricted line communities, 114-117, 120; challenges of assigning officers in the early 1980s when family issues were involved, 116-117;

placement of minority individuals, 117-118; impact in the early 1980s of a zero-tolerance drug policy, 119; matching of manpower requirements with billet levels, 119-120; in the early 1980s, Vice Admiral William Lawrence, the superintendent of the Naval Academy, took care of getting his own commandant of midshipmen, 121-122; Fran Galbraith was a civilian employee with a great deal of expertise on Navy flag matters, 122; congressional involvement in the early 1980s in Navy personnel assignments, 123-124; issues involved in the detailing process, 125-126 efforts by John F. Lehman, Jr., to control personnel assignments while serving in the early 1980s as Secretary of the Navy, 135-136; difficulties in the early 1980s in providing crews for the reactivated battleships of the Iowa (BB-61) class, 136-137

Naval Postgraduate School, Monterey, California
In the mid-1960s had a demanding curriculum for the officer students, 60-61

Navigation
In the mid-1950s student pilots at Hutchinson, Kansas, learned aerial navigation, 19-20; radio navigation in the late 1950s when weather required the use of instruments by aviators, 27; in the 1980s the Defense Mapping Agency was involved in terrain mapping to provide guidance for Tomahawk missiles, 149

North American Air Defense Command
Contacts in the early 1980s with the National Military Command Center concerning threat warnings, 130-131, 133

Okinawa
In the mid-1960s a group of officers from the air group of the aircraft carrier Bennington (CVS-20) wreaked havoc in a club at White Beach, 45; in the mid-1960s had the ashore headquarters of Patrol Force Seventh Fleet, 51-52

Oliver, Lieutenant Commander Daniel T., USN
In the late 1970s inspected a squadron in Patrol Wing Five and found it to be deficient in leadership, 104-105

OP-594
In the mid-1970s dealt with antisubmarine warfare readiness and training, 83-86

Osborn, Rear Admiral Oakley E., USN (Ret.)
Boyhood in the 1930s and 1940s on a farm in Nebraska, 1-8; parents of, 1-3, 6-9; siblings, 1, 3-4, 14; children of, 4, 8, 13, 34, 51, 110, 152-153; college education in the 1950s at the University of Nebraska and Colorado A&M, grandchildren of, 4, 11-12, 153; 6-7; wife Cathy, 8, 18, 20, 34-35, 51, 150-152; in 1955 joined the Navy after seeing a recruiting billboard, 8-9; from 1955 to 1957 took part in Aviation Officer Candidate School and then flight training and operational training, 9-20; from 1957 to 1961 served in Patrol Squadron 17, 23-36; in 1961-64 served in Patrol Squadron 31 as flight instructor, 36-40, 53-54, 58-59; in 1964-65 was aide and flag lieutenant to Commander Anti-Submarine Warfare Group Five, 40-50, 104; in

1965-66 was on the staff of Commander Patrol Force Seventh Fleet, 50-59; in 1966-67 was a student at the Naval Postgraduate School, 59-61; in 1967 attended a course in POW survival at Warner Springs, California, 61-65; from 1968 to 1970 served as pilot and department head in Patrol Squadron 19, 65-73; in 1970-71 was a student at the Army Command and General Staff College at Fort Leavenworth, Kansas, 73-75, 134-135; from 1971 to 1973 was XO and CO of Patrol Squadron 40, 76-82; served 1974-76 as ASW readiness and training officer in OpNav, 83-94; served 1976-78 as executive assistant to the Director of ASW and Ocean Surveillance, 94-103; from 1970 to 1980 was Commander Patrol Wing Five, 104-113; duty in 1980-82 in the Naval Military Personnel Command, 113-127, 135-137; elation upon being selected for flag rank, 127-128; brief service in 1982 in OP-01, 128-129; served from 1982 to 1984 as deputy director for operations in the National Military Command Center, 129; served 1984-86 as Commander Patrol Wings Pacific Fleet, 137-146; tour from 1986 to 1988 as Deputy Director, Defense Mapping Agency, 146-150; post-retirement activities, 150-153

P2V/P-2 Neptune
Flown in the mid-1950s at Hutchinson, Kansas, for multi-engine flight training, 19-20; deployments in the late 1950s of Patrol Squadron 17 aircraft, 23-29, 31-32; composition of a plane crew in the late 1950s, 29, 77; capabilities of the plane for various missions, 29-31; in the mid 1960s supported Market Time patrols off the coast of Vietnam, 52, 54-55

P-3 Orion
In the early 1960s was phased into the fleet with Patrol Squadron 31 serving as the Pacific Fleet readiness training squadron, 36-38; much more capable than its predecessor, the P2V Neptune, 37, 59; in 1963 planes from Patrol Squadron 31 made a long-distance flight to the Western Pacific, 37-38; change in missions over the years, 38, 108; in the mid-1980s some Japanese P-3s flew from Japan to California via Adak, Alaska, 49; in the mid 1960s supported Market Time patrols off the coast of Vietnam, 52, 54-55; evolution of the P-3 flight crew, 77-78; as commander of Patrol Wings Pacific Fleet in 1971-72, Rear Admiral Edward Waller developed a structured program for ASW crew training, 106; in July 1979 VP-23 was the first squadron to fire an operational Harpoon missile from a P-3 aircraft, 107-108; the P-3 is a good aircraft to operate in ice and snow, 112; in the mid-1980s, as Commander Patrols Wings Pacific Fleet, Osborn put a great emphasis on safety, 137-138, 141-142

P-5 Marlin
In the mid-1960s this seaplane flew in support of Operation Market Time off the coast of Vietnam, 52-55; in the 1960s the P-5s were old and difficult to support, so they were phased out, 58-59

Paisley, Melvyn R.
Was involved in questionable dealings during his tenure in the 1980s as Assistant Secretary of the Navy, 135-136

Patrol Force Seventh Fleet
In the mid-1960s operated as Task Force 72 of the Seventh Fleet, with headquarters rotating among three seaplane tenders and a base ashore in Okinawa, 51-52, 56-57; ran patrol plane support of Operation Market Time and Yankee Station off the coast of Vietnam, 52-55; the staff made plans for possible mining of North Vietnam, 57-58

Patrol Squadron 17 (VP-17)
In the late 1950s, while flying P2V Neptunes, was based at Whidbey Island and deployed to the Western Pacific, 23-26, 31-35; in the late 1950s experienced a variety of command leadership, 25-26; late 1950s deployment to the difficult weather and flying conditions of Alaska, 26-29, 33-34, 69; camaraderie within the squadron, 28-29; limited antisubmarine capabilities, 29-30; conducted reconnaissance flights looking for Soviet ships, 29, 31-34; originally designated as attack Mining Squadron Ten and did limited mine-warfare missions, 31; the survival suits worn by squadron air crews were of dubious value, 32-33

Patrol Squadron 19 (VP-19)
In the late 1960s won a lot of awards, but the squadron pilots soon left the service, 65-66; deployment to Adak, Alaska, included surveillance flights to track Soviet submarines, 66-73

Patrol Squadron 23 (VP-23)
In July 1979 VP-23 was the first squadron to fire an operational Harpoon missile from a P-3 aircraft, 107-108

Patrol Squadron 31 (VP-31)
In the early 1960s was the Pacific Fleet readiness training squadron for the new P-3 Orion, 36-37; in 1963 took the P-3 on a long-distance flight to the Western Pacific, 37-38; in the early 1960s demonstrated a home-made ASW trainer to the CNO, Admiral George Anderson, when he visited the aircraft carrier Kitty Hawk (CVA-63) at North Island, 53-54; in the early 1960s did some operations with P-5 Marlins, 58-59

Patrol Squadron 40 (VP-40)
In the early 1970s experienced a dramatic improvement in capability under the leadership of Commander Jack Weir, 76-77; evolution of the P-3 flight crew, 77-78; Osborn had to fire a couple of officers who lied about an engine problem in their plane, 78-79; issues for families of squadron members, 80; disciplinary matters, 80-81; impact of CNO Admiral Elmo Zumwalt's Z-grams, 81; a black pilot in the squadron did not perform as well as expected, 82

Patrol Wing Five
In the late 1970s one of the squadrons within the wing had serious leadership problems, 104-105; management of the individual squadrons by the patrol wing, 106, 108-109; in July 1979 VP-23 was the first squadron to fire an operational Harpoon

missile from a P-3 aircraft, 107-108; missions of the squadrons were ASW and ocean surveillance, 108; successful operations against Soviet submarines in the late 1970s, 112-113

Patrol Wings Pacific Fleet
In the mid-1980s U.S., Australian, and Japanese aircraft took part in international ASW exercises, 49, 68; as commander of the organization in 1971-72, Rear Admiral Edward Waller developed a structured program for ASW crew training, 106; in the mid-1980s, as commander of the force, Osborn put a great emphasis on safety, 137-138, 141-142; scope of the command, 142-143; disciplinary action against an officer for sexual misconduct, 143-144; Lieutenant Walter M. Kreitler, a gregarious individual, did a fine job as Osborn's aide, 146

Pay and Allowances
For many years TacAir aviators did not get per diem pay during deployments, whereas their patrol plane counterparts did, 39, 92

Pensacola, Florida, Naval Air Station
In the mid-1950s was the site of various phases of flight training for fledging naval aviators, 16-18

Personnel
Role of the Naval Military Personnel Command in the early 1980s in placing naval officers in a variety of billets in the staff corps and the various restricted line communities, 114-117, 120; challenges of assigning officers in the early 1980s when family issues were involved, 116-117; placement of minority individuals, 117-118; impact in the early 1980s of a zero-tolerance drug policy, 119; matching of manpower requirements with billet levels, 119-120; in the early 1980s, Vice Admiral William Lawrence, the superintendent of the Naval Academy, took care of getting his own commandant of midshipmen, 121-122; Fran Galbraith was a civilian employee with a great deal of expertise on Navy flag matters, 122; congressional involvement in the early 1980s in Navy personnel assignments, 123-124; issues involved in the detailing process, 125-126 efforts by John F. Lehman, Jr., to control personnel assignments while serving in the early 1980s as Secretary of the Navy, 135-136; difficulties in the early 1980s in providing crews for the reactivated battleships of the Iowa (BB-61) class, 136-137

Philippine Islands
In the Cubi Point officers' club in the mid-1960s naval aviators on liberty in Subic Bay were involved in inappropriate behavior, 46

Powell, General Colin, USA
Former Chairman of the Joint Chiefs of Staff who provided lessons for living, 75-76

Prisoners of War
   In 1967 Osborn attended a survival school in Warner Springs, California, to prepare him for the possibility of being captured as a prisoner of war, 61-65

Public Affairs
   Osborn has a low opinion of the way the Navy's Office of Information often handles public affairs issues, 120-121

Racial Issues
   In the early 1980s the Naval Military Personnel Command sometimes assigned minority individuals to jobs for which they were not sufficiently qualified, 117-118

Radio
   Radio navigation in the late 1950s when weather required the use of instruments by aviators, 27

Reeve, Robert C.
   Aviator who flew in the Aleutians during World War II and later formed an airline there, 28, 69

Reich, Rear Admiral Eli T., USN (USNA, 1935)
   In the mid-1960s served as Commander Anti-Submarine Warfare Group Five, based on board the aircraft carrier Bennington (CVS-20), 50

Replenishment at Sea
   In October 1965 Anti-Submarine Warfare Group Five had refueling difficulties when it ran into a typhoon while en route from the Western Pacific to California, 49-50

Roosevelt, Franklin D.
   As President in the early 1940s, manipulated the truth to aid the Allied war effort, 14-15

Rosenberg, Major General Robert A., USAF
   In the late 1980s, as director of the Defense Mapping Agency, set about to reduce the bloated structure of the organization, 146-147

Russell, Admiral James S., USN (USNA, 1926)
   After his retirement, visited Alaska to tell active-duty patrol plane pilots of his World War II experiences in the Aleutians, 27-28

Ryan, Vice Admiral Commander John R., USN (USNA, 1967)
   In the late 1970s did an outstanding job while serving as administrative officer for Commander Patrol Wing Five, 110-111; success in later billets, 111

S-3 Viking
Antisubmarine warfare aircraft that was introduced to the fleet in the mid-1970s, concurrently with corresponding simulators for training, 83-84, 86; in the 1990s the plane's ASW role was replaced by its service as a tanker, 91

SH-3 Sea King
Helicopter that was used primarily in a logistics role while on board the aircraft carrier Bennington (CVS-20) in the mid-1960s, 44

SNJ Texan
Aircraft used in the mid-1950s for training flights from Pensacola Naval Air Station, 16-17

Safety
The role of the Naval Air Training and Operations Procedures System (NATOPS) in promoting aviation safety, 87-88; in the mid-1980s, as Commander Patrol Wings Pacific Fleet, Osborn put a great emphasis on safety, 137-138, 141-142

Schaufelberger, Captain Albert A., Jr., USN (Ret.) (USNA, 1971)
In May 1983 sought information from the National Military Command Center concerning the death of his son in El Salvador, 132-133

Schaufelberger, Lieutenant Commander Albert A. III, USN (USNA, 1971)
In May 1983, while on duty as deputy commander of the U.S. military assistance advisory group in El Salvador, was shot and killed, 130, 132-133

Seventh Fleet, U.S.
In the mid-1960s Patrol Force Seventh Fleet operated as Task Force 72, with headquarters rotating among three seaplane tenders and a base ashore in Okinawa, 51-52; CTF 72 ran patrol plane support of Operation Market Time and Yankee Station off the coast of Vietnam, 52-55

Sexual Issues
In the mid-1980s the commanding officer of a Pacific Fleet patrol squadron was court-martialed because of a sexual misconduct with a female intelligence officer in the squadron, 143-144

Shear, Admiral Harold E., USN (USNA, 1942)
Even after he became Vice Chief of Naval Operations in 1975, kept a very close hand in his former specialty in antisubmarine warfare, 100; working style, 101-102

Simulators
In the late 1950s Patrol Squadron 17 used Link simulators to prepare for difficult flying conditions in Alaska, 27; use of flight simulators in the mid-1970s for training, 83-87

Sinz, Lieutenant Commander James P., USN
Officer who became an effective writer under Osborn's tutelage, 72-73

Sixth Fleet, U.S.
Successful operations against Soviet submarines in the Mediterranean in the late 1970s, 112-113; in 1986 Vice Admiral Kendall E. Moranville received a letter of reprimand for improprieties while he was serving as Commander Sixth Fleet, 145-146

Sonar
Development in the 1970s of dedicated ships to operated towed sonar arrays, 98; successful operations against Soviet submarines in the late 1970s, 112-113

Sonobuoys
Used in the late 1950s and early 1960s by the P2V Neptunes of Patrol Squadron 17 for submarine detection, 30

SOSUS (Sound Surveillance System)
Use of in the 1960s and 1980s for the tracking of Soviet submarines in the Pacific, 59, 67-68, 138-141; use of depth charges in 1958 to determine later locations for SOSUS arrays, 69; contribution to U.S. ASW capability in the 1970s, 102; successful operations against Soviet submarines in the late 1970s, 112-113

Soviet Navy
In the 1960s and 1980s U.S. Naval patrol planes and SOSUS tracked Soviet submarines operating in the Pacific, 67-68, 138-140; Soviet naval exercise in the mid-1980s, 68, 138-141; successful U.S. operations against Soviet submarines in the late 1970s, 112-113

Soviet Union
In the late 1950s Patrol Squadron 17 conducted reconnaissance flights looking for Soviet ships, 29, 31-34; Soviet fighter aircraft attacked some American patrol planes, 32; used range instrumentation ships for missile shots, 33; missile shots in the early 1980s, 131; in September 1983 a Soviet fighter plane short down a Korean airliner with 269 people on board, 131, 133

Stilwell, Lieutenant General Richard G., USA (Ret.) (USMA, 1938)
In the early 1980s played the role of the President in a command post exercise that simulated the reaction to a nuclear attack, 133

Subic Bay, Philippines
In the Cubi Point officers' club in the mid-1960s naval aviators on liberty were involved in inappropriate behavior, 46; good liberty spot during the Vietnam War, 47

Survival School
    In 1967 Osborn attended a survival school in Warner Springs, California, to prepare him for the possibility of being captured as a prisoner of war, 61-65

T-28 Trojan
    Aircraft used in the mid-1950s for instrument training at Pensacola Naval Air Station, 16

T-34 Mentor
    Aircraft used in the mid-1950s for instrument training at Pensacola Naval Air Station, 16-17

Tailhook Scandal
    In 1991, as the annual convention of the Tailhook Association in Las Vegas, male naval aviators were involved in a variety of forms of inappropriate behavior toward women, 46-47; the case was a public affairs disaster, 120

Tomahawk Missile
    In the 1980s the Defense Mapping Agency was involved in terrain mapping to provide guidance for Tomahawk missiles, 149

Training
    In 1955 at Aviation Officer Candidate School, 9-15; flight training and operational training in the mid-1950s, 16-18; multi-engine training in the mid-1950s at Hutchinson, Kansas, 19-20; in the late 1950s Patrol Squadron 17 used Link simulators to prepare for difficult flying conditions in Alaska, 27; in the early 1960s VP-31 was the Pacific Fleet readiness training squadron for the new P-3 Orion, 36-38; in 1967 Osborn attended a survival school in Warner Springs, California, to prepare him for the possibility of being captured as a prisoner of war, 61-65; in the early 1970s the Army Command and General Staff College, Fort Leavenworth, Kansas, provided staff training for officers from various services and foreign countries, 73-75; use of flight simulators in the mid-1970s for training, 83-87; role of the fleet replacement squadrons in aviation training, 87-88; development of computer programs in the mid-1970s for self-paced training of individuals, 93; as commander of Patrol Wings Pacific Fleet in 1971-72, Rear Admiral Edward Waller developed a structured program for ASW crew training, 106

VP-17
    See: Patrol Squadron 17 (VP-17)

VP-19
    See: Patrol Squadron 19 (VP-19)

VP-23
    See: Patrol Squadron 23 (VP-23)

VP-31
See: Patrol Squadron 31 (VP-31)

VP-40
See: Patrol Squadron 40 (VP-40)

Vietnam War
During the war Osborn's brother Clif harbored draft dodgers in Kansas, 3; in the mid-1960s ASW carriers deployed to the Tonkin Gulf, but there was virtually no submarine threat there, 44; in the mid-1960s Commander Patrol Force Seventh Fleet ran patrol plane support of Operation Market Time and Yankee Station off the coast of Vietnam, 52-55; in the mid-1960s the staff of Patrol Force Seventh Fleet made plans for possible mining of North Vietnam, 57-58; in 1967 Osborn attended a survival school in Warner Springs, California, to prepare him for the possibility of being captured as a prisoner of war, 61-65

Waller, Vice Admiral Edward C. III, USN (USNA, 1949)
In the mid-1970s held positions in the Pentagon in the OpNav antisubmarine warfare arena, 93-103; working style, 96, 103; as commander of Patrol Wings Pacific Fleet in 1971-72, Waller developed a structured program for ASW crew training, 106

Weather
Varying conditions in Alaska make for difficult flying, 26-27, 69-71; in the late 1950s Navy Patrol Squadron 17 flew ice reconnaissance flights out of Eielson Air Force Base in Alaska, 33-34; in October 1965 Anti-Submarine Warfare Group Five ran into a typhoon while en route from the Western Pacific to California, 49-50; winter weather sometimes makes Brunswick, Maine, Naval Air Station a difficult place from which to operate aircraft, 112

Weir, Commander Jack Tex, USN
In the early 1970s, as commanding officer of Patrol Squadron 40, dramatically improved its capability, 76-77

Wheatley, Commander John P., USN
In the late 1950s, as commanding officer of Patrol Squadron 17, prepared his pilots for the conditions they would face in Alaska, 26-27

Whidbey Island Naval Air Station, Washington
In the late 1950s served as the home base for P2V Neptunes and A3D Skywarriors, 23, 35

Wilkinson, Captain Edward A., Jr., USN (USNA, 1955)
In the late 1970s, when he commanded Patrol Wing Five, one of his squadrons had major deficiencies, 104-105

Wolkensdorfer, Rear Admiral Daniel J., USN
 In the 1980s, while serving as Commander Patrol Wings Pacific Fleet, declined to take action in a case of sexual misconduct on the part of officers in one of the squadrons in the command, 143-144

Zech, Vice Admiral Lando W., Jr., USN (USNA, 1945)
 Working style while serving in the early 1980s as Chief of Naval Personnel, 129

www.ingramcontent.com/pod-product-compliance
Lightning Source LLC
Chambersburg PA
CBHW080612170426
43209CB00007B/1415